FIT BODIES
FAT MINDS

Hourglass Books are for all who long for reformation and revival within the evangelical community. As "tracts for the times" they raise major issues of the day. Each book is serious in tone and probing in style but practical rather than academic, more often a first word than the last. Designed not only to be read but discussed and acted on, Hourglass Books are for all who seek to restore the gospel to evangelicals and evangelicals to the gospel.

Books in the series:

- *Dining with the Devil: The Megachurch Movement Flirts with Modernity* by Os Guinness
- *The Evangelical Forfeit: Can We Recover?* by John Seel
- *Restoring the Good Society: A New Vision for Politics and Culture* by Don E. Eberly
- *Haunted Houses: Ghostwriting and Religious Publishing* by Edward E. Plowman (forthcoming)
- *Power Encounters: Reclaiming Spiritual Warfare* by David Powlison (forthcoming)

OS GUINNESS

FIT BODIES
FAT MINDS

Why Evangelicals
Don't Think
and
What to Do About It

HOURGLASS BOOKS

Baker Books

A Division of Baker Book House Co
Grand Rapids, Michigan 49516

Acknowledgments

With deep gratitude to Amy Boucher, Peter Edman, Mark Filiatreau, and Virginia Mooney, without whose skills and support this book would have been impossible to write in the midst of a hectic schedule. And to my old friend David Wells, whose keen reading was an invaluable source of correction and wisdom.

© 1994 by Os Guinness

Library of Congress Cataloging-in-Publication Data

Guinness, Os
    Fit bodies, fat minds : why evangelicals don't think and what to do about it / Os Guinness.
        p.   cm.
    Includes bibliographical references.
    ISBN 0-8010-3870-7
    1. Evangelicalism—United States. 2. United States—Intellectual life. I. Title.
BR526.G86   1994
277.3'082—dc20   94-29324

"KUDZU" by Doug Marlette used by permission of Doug Marlette and Creators Syndicate.

Scripture quotations taken from the *Holy Bible, New International Version.* Copyright © 1973, 1978, 1984 by International Bible Society.

ISBN: 0-8010-3870-7

Third printing, February 1995

Printed in the United States of America

D.O.M

and to Donald J. Drew

who first taught me to think and to think Christianly,
first introduced me to Shakespeare and the world of literature,
first encouraged me in public speaking,
and first urged me to write a book—
a peerless teacher and true friend.

CONTENTS

KUDZU

© 1993 Doug Marlette

INTRODUCTION

A SCANDAL AND A SIN

"I WANT TO ASK YOU MY $64,000 QUESTION. It's something I've asked each speaker at the sessions I've attended."

There was an audible gasp. A rush of attention swept the room. It was partly because the other speakers included many of the big names of American Christendom. It was partly too in anticipation of the question. Would it be about the meaning of life, the problem of evil, the state of the world, or simply the headline of the day? But the interest was also because of the questioner. Slim, svelte, and tanned, she was a striking blond in her late twenties who would clearly look just as much at home on a California beach as in the packed seminar room in Orange County.

"How's your body?" she blurted out.

Somewhat taken aback at her $64,000 question, I was silent for a few seconds and then—almost without thinking—replied:

"Madame, I'm English. How's your mind?"

There was a roar of laughter, in which she joined, and the questions immediately swung back to subjects more important than my body and her mind. But the incident lingered with me. Coming after a serious speech in a serious Christian convention, it jolted me to consider a leading problem in American evangelicalism—anti-intellectualism.

Anti-intellectualism is a disposition to discount the importance of truth and the life of the mind. Living in a sensuous culture and an increasingly emotional democracy, American evangelicals in the last generation have simultaneously toned up their bodies and dumbed down their minds. The result? Many suffer from a modern form of what the ancient stoics called "mental hedonism"—having fit bodies but fat minds.

This contemporary form of anti-intellectualism fits perfectly with the German philosopher Friedrich Nietzsche's prediction of the arrival of "the last man" (and woman). Secular people, losing touch with transcendence, would eventually lose a reference point from which to look down and judge themselves. In the end they would lose even the capacity to despise themselves. Thus because of "the death of God" they would confuse heaven with happiness and happiness with health.

Nietzsche's description in *Thus Spake Zarathustra* is the perfect parody of the joggers and dieters' America of the late twentieth century. Health has replaced both heaven and ethics. Athleticism is the new form of asceticism. Positive thinking is prized above reflection and meditation. Human experience, with its rich, tragic, and ironic complexities, is scaled down to the glow of physical well-being. And self-knowledge, self-mastery, and self-fulfillment are promised through exercise and eating right. "One has one's little pleasure for the day and one's little pleasure for the night," Nietzsche commented. "But one has a regard for health. 'We have invented happiness,' say the last men, and they blink."[1]

Modern attitudes about health and happiness are only one factor shaping contemporary anti-intellectualism. Other factors, which we will examine later, are such diverse influences as advertising, television, talk shows, and virtual reality. But for American evangelicals anti-intellectualism is much older than any of these recent forces. Its importance, too, is far deeper.

At root, evangelical anti-intellectualism is both a scandal and a sin. It is a scandal in the sense of being an offense and a stumbling block that needlessly hinders serious people from considering the Christian faith and coming to Christ. It is a sin because it is a refusal, contrary to the first of Jesus' two great commandments, to love the Lord our God with our minds. As Ambassador Charles Malik warned in his incisive address at the dedication of the Billy Graham Center at Wheaton College in 1980, speaking as an Orthodox believer to evangelicals, "I must be frank with you: the greatest danger besetting American Evangelical Christianity is the danger of anti-intellectualism. The mind as to its greatest and deepest reaches is not cared for enough."[2]

As such, we evangelicals need to examine our anti-intellectualism, confess its pervasiveness, repent of its wrongness, and seek God's restoration to live up to our name—truly being people of the gospel who love God not only with our hearts, souls, and strength, but also with our minds. There are many other parts of evangelicalism in dire need of reformation, but the plea for a reformation in Christian thinking is the message of this book.

THE THIRD ALARM BELL

The incident described above was admittedly trivial, but it set off an alarm bell that rang as if for the third time in my life. The alarm rang first when I read Harry Blamires's *The Christian Mind*, published in 1963. I was a student at London University and somewhat new as a follower of Christ. Like many then, I felt challenged and excited to relate my faith in Christ to the turbulent but heady days of "swinging London" and the wider seismic sixties.

To many young Christians like me, Blamires's words were blunt but bracing. "We speak of 'the modern mind' and of 'the scientific mind,' using that word *mind* of a collectively accepted set of notions and attitudes. On the pattern of such usage I have posited a Christian Mind, chiefly for the purpose of showing it does not exist." Blamires continued, "There is no longer a Christian Mind. . . . The Christian Mind has succumbed to the secular drift with a degree of weakness unmatched in Christian History."[3]

Blamires's analysis needed no confirmation in the world of the universities of that day. Both in Europe and the United States secularism was dominant and domineering. "God," the logical positivist philosophers crowed, was less meaningful as a word than "dog." Not surprisingly many Christians concluded that caution was the better part of valor. They kept their heads low and gained a name for ducking the big questions and the real issues. As the aging philosopher Bertrand Russell mocked, "Most Christians would rather die than think—in fact they do."

But Blamires's call did not go unheeded. Picked up by young evangelicals, the challenge to develop a Christian mind and to "think Christianly" grew into a significant movement. Among its lasting results were a stream of superb books published by such evangelical houses as InterVarsity Press and the foundation of such centers as Regent College in Vancouver, the London Institute for Contemporary Christianity, New College in Berkeley, and the Zadok Centre in Canberra, Australia.

Yet overall the movement did not live up to its early expectations. Most of the colleges and study centers were swimming upstream, fighting theological and economic currents that threatened to sideline or submerge them. Thinking Christianly in the modern world, it was said, was utopian and impossible. Besides, said those below, it was "elitist." On the contrary, said those above, it was "simplistic" and "popularizing," a travesty of true scholarship. (As broadcaster Alistair Cooke has observed, the term "popularizing" in America is "a horrid word implying a degradation of truth in the interests of fat royalties, public popularity, or an invitation to appear on television."[4]) Above all, the movement never proved more than a minority interest. It touched only a tiny stream of evangelical hopefuls. The broad river of the wider evangelical movement rolled on uncomprehending and unconcerned.

The second time the alarm bell rang for me was in 1976. I was reading an article in *The New York Review of Books* by John Schaar, professor of political science at the University of Santa Cruz. The year 1976 had been called "the year of the evangelical." After mostly missing out on the sixties, evangelicals woke up abruptly in the seventies, mainly through the catalytic events of 1973—Watergate, *Roe v. Wade*, and the OPEC crisis. With the convergence in 1976 of Jimmy Carter's election to the presidency and the publication of Charles Colson's best-selling story, *Born Again*, a new moment in national life beckoned to evangelicals. The Protestant mainline was sidelined, as the saying went. Roman Catholics had not yet flexed their muscles in public as they have since then. Evangelicals, with their long history and broad numbers, could reclaim a position of national influence as the rightful heirs of America's "first faith."

But John Schaar argued otherwise. He stated that evangelicals would have no lasting influence because the old lesson had not been learned. Evangelicals still had no Christian mind. What Americans were seeing in 1976, Schaar claimed, was a revival in evangelicalism, but there was not the slightest possibility that it could lead to a national renaissance too. He continued:

> Nor is there much likelihood that leaders of evangelical opinion will develop any significant new vision of public life and policy. The brute fact remains that this country, which has produced more Protestant believers than any other, has also produced fewer powerful Protestant theologians and theological-social theorists than any other major Protestant country. The evangelical leaders are not equipped intellectually to think through the complex social issues of the times and offer genuinely new and promising solutions to them. . . . Without a genuinely critical position resting on Christian foundations and directed by a coherent theological vision that can deal with modern science and technology and the reality of foreign cultures, it is very likely that the evangelical voice in politics today will once again confuse the Christian faith with the American flag.[5]

Nearly two decades later, Schaar's predictions can be read as an epitaph on evangelical renewal in general and the ineffectiveness of the Christian Right in particular. Magnificent exceptions can be found and a myriad of reasons can be used as an excuse—the widely cited "hostility" of the "media elite" being a current favorite. But many of the deeper reasons for the general evangelical failure are rooted in the lack of a distinctive Christian mind. Failing to think Christianly, evangelicals have been forced into the role of cultural imitators and adapters rather than originators. In biblical terms, it is to be worldly and conformist, not decisively Christian.

RIPE FOR REFORM

The third alarm bell rang for me in the woman's question, but this time with an extra urgency. Evangelicals are facing their "Sputnik moment" in the sense that cultural challenges confront us today as the launching of the Soviet satellite confronted America in 1957. Sputnik in the late fifties underscored the fact that discounting the mind is not only a disgrace but a hazard to survival.

The challenge is before us. On the one hand, the deepening consequences of a lack of a Christian mind are ever more apparent in evangelicalism. On the other hand, the alternatives to reform are starker and the excuses for inaction less convincing. In short, the time is ripe for repentance and reform as a key part of restoring the gospel to evangelicals and evangelicals to the gospel.

Critics of evangelical anti-intellectualism commonly cite four great facts of our shame. First, no general evangelical magazine of serious ideas exists. Second, no cogent case for the Christian faith has been written by a living evangelical that can be confidently given to a serious non-Christian reader. Third, there is no evangelical university worthy of the name that has a program of graduate studies on a par with other major universities. Fourth, there has been no generally accepted, constructive formulation of an evangelical public philosophy for the last hundred years.

At its highest and most serious the scandal of evangelical anti-intellectualism goes beyond any such list or litany. A deliberate and deep-running anti-intellectualism is a prominent part of the wider evangelical crisis. Evangelicals justifiably regard themselves as heirs of America's "first faith," a movement that is not only numerous but has been highly influential and deeply American. Yet today extraordinary confusion and disarray surround the character of evangelicalism.

Does evangelicalism have a clear identity? Does it have a strong future? Dismissals that were once the watchword of critics and defectors now form the doubts of many evangelical leaders. For in one generation the evangelical movement has experienced a sea change: It has moved from being, in large part, confessionally defined to being a fraternity of institutions to being virtually a coalition of causes to being a movement in plain disarray. Worst of all, there is neither an agreed defining character of "evangelical" around which reformation and regrouping can occur nor any evident leadership willing or able to assert it.

Not surprisingly the disarray and frustration is deepest among evangelicals who think—whether those who do so for a living, such as academics, or those who do so for the love of it, such as artists. For the truth is, for those who think, the present state of American evangelicalism is appalling. As a spiritually and theologically defined community of faith, evangelicalism is weak or next to nonexistent; as a subculture, it is stronger but often embarrassing and downright offensive.

Evangelical anti-intellectualism bears directly on many of the problems of evangelicalism—superficial or bad theology, the lack of a serious apology for the faith, the lack of a constructive public philosophy, and the continued defections of thinking evangelicals in the direction of Catholicism or Eastern Orthodoxy. Catholics, by contrast, can boast of strengths that are alluring precisely because they coincide with evangelical weaknesses— for example, in regard to authority, tradition, liturgical worship, aesthetics, and a constructive public philosophy.

Two particular factors, in turn, lie behind evangelical ineffectiveness in public life. Both underscore the urgent need to recover an evangelical mind. One is the development of an "education gap" in American religion. In the past Christian believers have spanned the full range of intelligence and education in American life—education and intelligence having no necessary link, needless to say. For various reasons, however, a fateful gap has grown since the 1960s. Those more educated now tend to be significantly less religious; those more religious tend to be significantly less educated. For example, evangelicals are the only religious group in America that exceeds the national average of those not completing the eighth grade or high school. At the same time only 24.2 percent of evangelicals achieve some university training, compared with 68 percent of non-Christians.[6]

This education gap is a critical factor in creating an odd situation. As Peter L. Berger points out, the United States is distinctive among modern nations for having a populace as religious as India's but an elite as secular as Sweden's. Evangelicals who have failed to think Christianly in this era of the so-called "knowledge elite" and the "information explosion" have taken themselves out of the running for natural influence in culture. No amount of complaining about "the hostility of the elites" can alter the largely self-chosen evangelical banishment.

The other factor is the lack of an evangelical public philosophy, or common vision for the common good. Historian Mark Noll points out the lack of an evangelical public philosophy since William Jennings Bryan—in other words, for the best part of a most critical century. Again, there are exceptions, such as the Williamsburg Charter, which celebrated the bicentennial of the U.S. Constitution, set out a distinctive public philosophy, and had critical evangelical contributions. But the general point holds true. I remember well a Washington journalist saying to me in 1989, "Why did you use the words 'evangelical public philosophy'? They're either empty or a contradiction in terms. Today's evangelicals are nothing but partisan and sectarian."

Much more is at stake than public relations or national standing. Without a public philosophy that defends the common good, outsiders tend to view evangelicals' public involvement as constitutionally legitimate but intrusive and unwelcome.

For example, among leadership groups in the 1980s—business leaders, government leaders, academics, priests, and rabbis—evangelicals were perceived as the greatest "threat to democracy." Thirty-four percent of academics rated evangelicals as a menace to democracy, compared with only 14 percent who saw any danger from racists, the Ku Klux Klan, or Nazis.[7]

Without a clear commitment to a common vision for the common good, evangelicals are vulnerable to the charge that we are tribespeople rather than citizens—or as the charge has been leveled, that our real concern is not justice but "just us."

These two factors—the growth of the education gap in faith and the lack of a public philosophy—lie behind evangelical ineffectiveness in public life. They result directly from the lack of a Christian mind. They reinforce some of the strategic errors evangelicals have made repeatedly in recent public initiatives:

First, evangelicals have concentrated their power in the peripheries of modern society rather than the center. Whereas, for example, the Jewish community has concentrated its strength wisely and strategically in such cities as New York, Los Angeles, and Chicago, evangelicals have chosen to do so in less strategic centers, such as Wheaton, Colorado Springs, and Orlando. The 1977 shift of the *Christianity Today* office from Washington, D.C., to Carol Stream, Illinois, is the epitome of this attitude.

Second, evangelicals have relied on populist strengths and rhetoric rather than addressing the gatekeepers of modern society—those whose positions of office or responsibility enable them to stand at the doorways of public power and influence. This reliance has been a defining feature and recurring weakness of evangelicals in the religious Right.

Third, evangelicals have sought to change society through politics rather than through changing the culture. Not only does this recent position reverse the traditional emphasis on transforming society through changing individuals, but it comes at a time when many people acknowledge that politics cannot touch many of the deepest crises in society. These crises are now termed cultural and "pre-political."

Fourth, evangelicals have chosen to rely on a rhetoric of protest, pronouncement, and picketing rather than persuasion. This is despite the fact that the nature of the gospel, the precedents of our history, and the challenges of contemporary pluralism combine to make the winning of hearts and minds an urgent priority.

Our current public ineffectiveness is only one example of how anti-intellectualism is a scandal as well as a sin—a genuine offense and a stumbling block that hinders outsiders from considering Christ and Christian claims. Properly understood, the scandalous character of anti-intellectualism is less important and more recent than its sinful character. But seen realistically, the overlap between the sense of scandal and the sense of sin creates an opportune moment to tackle the problem.

People who might never act against anti-intellectualism simply on the grounds that it is a sin are now being prodded into action because it is a scandal and a severe cultural handicap. Far better to think Christianly as a direct act of love for God. But better than not thinking at all is to think Christianly because not to do so is to court failure—and then discover that it is an act of love for God all along.

Beware Intellectuals

Needless to say, the sin of anti-intellectualism is deeper and older than the scandal. For anti-intellectualism is truly the refusal to love the Lord our God with our minds as required by the first of Jesus' commandments. Thus, if we take the commands of Jesus seriously, we cannot dismiss the charge of anti-intellectualism as elitism or intellectual snobbery. As God has given us minds, we can measure obedience by whether we are loving him with those minds, and disobedience by whether we are not.

Loving God with our minds is not finally a question of orthodoxy, but of love. Offering up our minds to God in all our thinking is a part of our praise. Anti-intellectualism is quite simply a sin. Evangelicals must address it as such, beyond all excuses, evasions, or rationalizations of false piety.

There are unquestionable dangers in this call to reform the Christian mind. First is the age-old pitfall concerning the principle of the matter. Mounting an attack on evangelical anti-intellectualism almost automatically releases a cloud of darkly unhelpful attitudes toward thinking. Anyone who makes such a call must be guilty of superiority, it is feared. Any who heed the call surely suffer from snobbery. All who resist the call are clearly victims of reverse-snobbery. Any who stand back detached because they have seen it all before are obviously guilty of cynicism. And so on and so on.

But hostility between people of ideas and ordinary people is at least as old as Western philosophy itself. Such tensions as highbrow versus lowbrow, town versus gown, elite versus masses, and eggheads versus fatheads are a contradiction of the harmony of the body of Christ. But evangelicals are no more immune from these tensions than anyone else.

We therefore need to affirm certain truths: Intellectualism is not the answer to anti-intellectualism, for the perils of intellectualism—supremely in gnosticism—are deadly and ever recurring.

Our passion is not for academic respectability, but for faithfulness to the commands of Jesus. Our lament is not for the destruction of the elite culture of Western civilization but for the deficiencies in our everyday discipleship as Christians. Our mission is not the recovery of some lost golden age of purportedly better Christian thinking but the renewal of a church today that has integrity, faithfulness, and effectiveness in its thinking. Once again thinking Christianly is first and foremost a matter of love—of minds in love with God and the truth of his world.

Second is a special new danger surrounding intellectuals and intellectualism. At the very moment of intellectuals' enhanced status and power in modern society—with intellectuals variously described as the "new class," "thought leaders," "gatekeepers," "opinion leaders," and the "ruling cognitariat"—they have a radically altered relationship to Western civilization. As historian Paul Johnson has analyzed, intellectuals in their earlier incarnations as priests and scribes were once guardians of culture. As such they were limited in their influence because they worked within the guidelines of tradition. Today, however, secular intellectuals are the self-styled tutors to humanity and guides to human progress. But no canons bind them except their own thinking. They are inspired solely by their own unaided intellects.

Johnson's portrayal of Western intellectuals from Jean-Jacques Rousseau in the eighteenth century to such twentieth-century thinkers as Jean-Paul Sartre and Lillian Hellman is sobering. They have been spoiled, vain, egoistic, self-publicizing, dishonest, deceptive, romantic about violence, prone to authoritarianism, lovers of humanity rather than real people, and heartless toward family and friends. This appalling record challenges the intellectuals' credentials to advise humanity on how to conduct its affairs. Our conclusion, Johnson says, can only be skepticism. "One of the principal lessons of our tragic century, which has seen so many innocent lives sacrificed in schemes to improve the lot of humanity, is—beware intellectuals."[8]

Third is a practical pitfall in any attack on anti-intellectualism. If the challenge remains all criticism and no action, it becomes self-defeating. By harping on the problem, we can easily highlight and reinforce the gap so that those on each side are more entrenched than ever. By endlessly analyzing the reasons for the gap, we can actually encourage people to rationalize their failure to bridge it. Criticism without action readily becomes self-fulfilling and self-defeating.

In the case of American evangelicals there is an added twist to these dangers. Not only is the problem of anti-intellectualism much older than most evangelicals realize, it is also a weakness that has grown out of strengths—strengths that have turned into a weakness. Worst of all, anti-intellectualism has become so much a part of the American evangelical identity—to evangelicals themselves as well as to observers—that to renounce it would seem like an act of suicide. Evangelicals and anti-intellectualism have gone together for so long that each seems unthinkable without the other. Anti-intellectualism is more than a set of notions that evangelicals have; it is a set of notions that we *are*.

This, however, is precisely the challenge of discipleship—giving up what seems like our very selves to find our true selves. It is also the challenge of reformation—difficult and daring at once—which we evangelicals face today. If we are to live up to our name as people who seek to define ourselves and our lives by the first things of the gospel, obedience to the first great commandment is not optional. To the extent God has given us minds, we must love God with all our minds and in all of our lives in a way that is shaped decisively by him.

PART ONE

A GHOST MIND

"I AGREE WITH WHAT YOU'RE SAYING, but don't you think you are being unfair? After all, it took Europe centuries before it developed the great centers of Christian learning, such as the Universities of the Sorbonne, Oxford, and Cambridge. America is a frontier society. Just give us time." That retort by an Ivy League college student represents a typical response to criticism of anti-intellectualism. Americans in general and evangelicals in particular are often quite defensive about the subject of anti-intellectualism—particularly when raised by outsiders.

This defensiveness typically takes two forms. One form, as in the response above, is to make plausible but false excuses. Is the Christian mind to be equated with a great university? Is it only the product of an advanced culture and settled conditions? The answer in both cases is no. Evangelicals are often surprised that one of the greatest examples of a Christian mind was at the very beginning of the American story when conditions were most precarious and least settled—the Puritan movement. For Christians, no past age is ever a Golden Age, but in this case the first is—thus far—the best.

WHEN RELIGION WAS THE ROAD TO KNOWLEDGE

Alexis de Tocqueville is often quoted in support of the genius of the framers of the American experiment. His observations in

22

the 1830s on the relationship of Puritan faith and learning in the 1650s are equally illuminating. "It is by the mandates relating to public education," Tocqueville noted, "that the original character of American civilization is at once placed in the clearest light." He then cites the illuminating preamble to the Puritan provision that every township should have a school—

> "Whereas," says the law, "Satan, the enemy of mankind, finds his strongest weapons in the ignorance of men, and whereas it is important that the wisdom of our fathers shall not remain buried in their tombs, and whereas the education of children is one of the prime concerns of the state, with the aid of the Lord. . . ."

Tocqueville's conclusion is a glorious tribute to the Christian mind of the Puritans: "In America religion is the road to knowledge and the observance of divine laws leads man to civil freedom."[1]

Religion as the road to knowledge? Ignorance as the weapon of Satan? An awareness of history in order to keep alive the wisdom of the fathers? Each of these themes would make an apt motto for different aspects of a campaign to reform the evangelical mind today. At the very least they are a bench mark to gauge how far we have declined.

The same commitment is abundantly clear in *New England's First Fruits* (1643), the Puritan explanation of what led to the founding of Harvard College:

> After God had carried us safe to *New England*, and wee had builded our houses, provided necessaries for our livelihood, rear'd convenient places for God's worship, and settled the Civil Government; One of the next things we longed for, and looked after was to advance *Learning* and perpetuate it to Posterity; dreading to have an illiterate Ministry to the Churches, when our present Ministers shall lie in the Dust."[2]

Historian Richard Hofstadter gives an equally ringing tribute to the Puritans in his classic work *Anti-Intellectualism in American Life*. Known for not mincing his words about the baleful influence of evangelicalism on thinking, he praises the Puritans. "It is doubtful that any community ever had more faith in the value of learning and intellect than Massachusetts Bay." Indeed, Hofstadter continues, citing an earlier historian,

> In its inception, New England was not an agricultural community, nor a manufacturing community, nor a trading community: it was a thinking community; an arena and mart for ideas; its characteristic organ being not the hand, nor the heart, nor the pocket, but the brain. . . . Probably no other community of pioneers ever so honored study, so reverenced the symbols and instruments of learning.[3]

There is no escaping the conclusion. Citing such factors as a lack of settled conditions is a false excuse. The Christian mind in America was never more remarkable than in its earliest days, when society was not settled and the conditions were hazardous and far from secure. To our shame it is the secular mind, not the Christian mind, that has expanded most fruitfully in the settled conditions of later times. There is a grand irony in the fact that we evangelicals are citizens in a republic whose revolution was led by intellectuals and are disciples in a community of faith whose reformation was led by intellectuals—yet we are the epitome of anti-intellectualism and proud of it.

HOW THE EAST WAS LOST

The second type of defensiveness is usually more sophisticated. Whereas the first hides behind false excuses, the second hides behind false explanations—explanations that simply do not explain what they purport to. Its characteristic strategy is to analyze the flow of ideas elaborately without explaining how these ideas affect ordinary people in ordinary situations. The snag is obvious: American anti-intellectualism is brazenly populist and ruggedly impervious to such high-flying ideas. The real explanation must lie elsewhere.

Such philosophical explanations are often true and useful when it comes to tracing the history of ideas, especially in their university setting. But as an explanation for common or garden anti-intellectualism these explanations are excessively European, intellectual, and conspiratorial. Although the Kantian and Nietzschean revolutions in ideas, for example, are immensely important, the late eighteenth-century evangelical farmer in Kentucky or the trader from Virginia were oblivious to such trends. They were marked by a characteristic populist anti-intellectualism long before Nietzsche was born or Kant's ideas arrived on America's shores. Our real need is for explanations of anti-intellectualism that are American and that touch the lives of ordinary people, not just the well-educated.

A better way to analyze evangelical anti-intellectualism—the path we will follow in this book—is to trace how it has been shaped in two long stages. The first phase, roughly from 1700 to the Civil War, is the story of the long, slow retreat from the Christian mind to the creation of a "ghost mind." We will examine this phase in Part One of this book. The second phase, from the Civil War to the present, is the story of the long, slow rise of a mass mind and the creation of an "idiot culture." This is the subject of Part Two. As we will see, this book analyzes evangelicalism, not fundamentalism. The latter originates in a different period and is influenced by added pressures not considered here.

What do I mean by "ghost mind"? In the early nineteenth century a consequence of the rapid frontier expansion was the creation of ghost towns and ghost colleges—towns and colleges left behind in the great rush west. In a similar way the story of the retreat from a Christian mind is the story of a number of influences raging like a fire through the evangelical movement. They have left in their wake a devastation of the earlier Puritan mind and thus the creation of a virtual ghost mind with few distinctively Christian strengths left.

Before examining these damaging trends (set out here in a simple way as eight Ps), I need to underscore several introductory points. First, I am not arguing that these trends undermined the

Puritan mind directly. The Puritan mind had effectively softened and caved in before the development of these trends. The trends therefore did little more than undermine what was left of the Puritan mind. The contrast between them and the Puritan mind, however, is illuminating for understanding the development of our anti-intellectualism.

Second, although we are looking at the destructive side of the trends, most of them also have a positive side. They were destructive in their eventual impact on the Christian mind, but they brought many benefits too—which, of course, was the reason they were a menace. As the trends were true and important in some ways, their damaging side passed—and often still passes—unnoticed.

Third, almost none of these trends can be blamed on hostile, outside malevolence. In the climate of America's contemporary "culture wars" the rhetoric of blaming and victim-playing is widespread. Everything is posed in terms of "we" and "they." The reason for our cultural impotence, for example, is described as the story of "the stealing of America."

But the story of evangelicalism prior to the Civil War does not fit such an analysis. Evangelicals, of course, had foes and rivals. Such great thinkers and writers as Thomas Jefferson and Tom Paine were hardly champions of any orthodox Christian faith. But the real damage to evangelicals was self-inflicted. As we shall see, evangelicals repeatedly hurt themselves by their chosen positions. Worse still, they gloried in their wounds. The true story of the evangelical mind in retreat is the story of the surrender, not the stealing, of America.

Fourth, although our emphasis here is on these trends in the period before the Civil War (in all but one case), all of them endure today in one form or another. These trends are not antiquarian or of interest only to historians. They shaped the evangelical mind when it was fluid and molten. For better or worse we live today with the molds they cast then.

Our challenge of reformation is to cast new and more biblical molds now. Put differently, many a home fellowship or campus group today displays features of thinking and non-thinking that cannot fully be explained by such modern factors as advertising, television, or attitudes about health and happiness—let alone the latest intellectual trends on today's campuses. Their origin lies in trends of a century and a half to two centuries ago that were constitutive of evangelicalism itself. Understanding those trends is the key to understanding ourselves now and seeing where we need reformation.

1

POLARIZATION

THE FIRST INFLUENCE THAT HELPED TO UNDERMINE what was left of the Puritan mind and leave its mark on evangelicalism is the polarization of truth, in the sense of a false antagonism between heart and mind. To be sure, no one in the fallen world—believer or unbeliever—has the capacity to hold God's truth in its entirety. As the Apostle Paul wrote to the Romans, the unbeliever "holds the truth in unrighteousness." If no unbeliever is totally wrong or completely evil—because the truth is inextinguishable—no believer has the full truth by the scruff of the neck. Holding the truth in a sinful manner, our grasp is always incomplete, however conscientious or hardworking we may be. In Martin Luther's picture, we are like a drunken peasant clambering onto his donkey from one side only to tumble off the other.

Some tension between mind and heart, intellect and emotions, is a recurring theme in Christian history. Yet despite this condition, a hallmark of the Puritan mind was its commitment to the unity of truth and thus to the integration of faith and life, worship and discipleship, faith and learning. All of these things were under the lordship of Christ. Each was part of its own sphere and calling. None was to be isolated or treated as a favored part of truth.

This feature was not unique to the Puritans—various periods and schools of Catholic thinking have had the same high aim. But for the early American Puritans it was a direct legacy of the

Calvinist wing of the Reformation as it passionately endeavored to return to the New Testament requirement of the lordship of Christ. As the great Calvinist prime minister and pastor Abraham Kuyper was to express it later in Holland, "There is not one square inch of the entire creation about which Jesus Christ does not cry out, 'This is mine! This belongs to me!' "[1]

A TALE OF TWO POLES

By the early eighteenth century and the time of the later Puritans, however, this passion was cooling and the old false antagonisms were developing—between faith and learning, learning and experience, formality and fervor, a sharp mind and a warm heart. Then when the First Great Awakening occurred, many people emphasized one of the two poles at the expense of the other—faith, with its warm heart, experience, and fervor usually being favored at the expense of learning and a sharp mind.

There were, of course, magnificent exceptions even then. Jonathan Edwards, for example, ranks as one of America's finest thinkers in his or any age. And his was a style of thinking rooted in worship and suffused with deep devotion, combining the old Puritan's regard for doctrine with the new revivalists' passion for deep experience.

But counterexamples multiplied and the false antagonisms appeared. One example was the tub-thumping preacher Gilbert Tennent who dismissed the older clergy concerned about orthodoxy as "Letter-learned and regular Pharisees."[2] Another was Bishop Francis Asbury, the eighteenth-century pioneering Methodist leader who published his book *Discipline* for his lay preachers in 1784. In it he poses a choice between the importance of study and the importance of soul-saving that would have been unthinkable to the Puritans. "If you can do but one, let your studies alone. I would throw by all the Libraries of the World rather than be guilty of the Loss of one Soul."[3] Or as his followers added later, "We have always been more anxious to preserve a living rather than a learned ministry."[4]

The false antagonisms of that sort of either/or thinking have become a standard feature of evangelicalism, sometimes with the question posed falsely and the answer chosen wrongly. More often we evangelicals choose a good thing but in a bad way because we choose at the expense of another good thing. In terms of a Christian mind, we evangelicals characteristically pit "heart" versus "head" and opt for heart as the more spiritual choice. We are like the Tin Woodman, in L. Frank Baum's *The Wonderful Wizard of Oz*, who chooses a heart rather than a head:

"Why didn't you walk around the hole?" asked the Tin Woodman.

"I don't know enough," replied the Scarecrow, cheerfully. "My head is stuffed with straw, you know, and that is why I am going to Oz to ask him for some brains."

"Oh, I see;" said the Tin Woodman. "But, after all, brains are not the best things in the world."

"Have you any?" enquired the Scarecrow.

"No, my head is quite empty," answered the Woodman; "but once I had brains, and a heart also; so having tried them both, I should much rather have a heart. . . ."

"All the same," said the Scarecrow, "I shall ask for brains instead of a heart; for a fool would not know what to do with a heart if he had one."

"I shall take the heart," returned the Tin Woodman; "for brains do not make one happy, and happiness is the best thing in the world."[5]

Many of us have come across spiritual versions of this falsely polarized thinking. I have often been in Christian fellowships on university campuses where the polarizing tendency was swift and automatic. After a half-hour discussion the group becomes as deeply split as if a leader had divided it in two. Usually those in favor of thinking Christianly find themselves pitted against those who are more "spiritual," "practical," "evangelistic," concerned with "social justice," or whatever the other worthy concern. Worst of all, those committed to think Christianly are not simply one among many groups in the discussion, but one against all the rest—and therefore obviously *un*spiritual, *im*practical, *un*concerned with evangelism, *un*caring about justice, and so on.

As Richard Hofstadter has pointed out, the case against the mind in America is commonly founded upon "a set of fictional and wholly abstract antagonisms"—intellect versus feeling, intellect versus character, intellect versus democracy, and so on.[6] The fallacy, of course, is that these fictional antagonisms are based not on the real limits of the mind but on "a simplified divorce of intellect from all other human qualities with which it may be combined."[7] Hofstadter concludes, "The evangelical movement has been the most powerful carrier of this kind of religious anti-intellectualism. . . ."[8]

Never mind that "heart" in the Bible is more a matter of understanding than sentiment—so "heart" versus "head" is a false choice. Never mind that the Spirit of truth is also the Spirit of love and the Spirit of power—so truth must never be pitted against love and power. Ever since the mid-eighteenth century we evangelicals have had a natural bias toward the Tin Woodman's choice—empty brains and happy hearts. We even glory in our choice.

LOSE THE MIND, LOSE THE WORLD?

Ironically, evangelicals are often much more aware of other forms of polarization—"conservative" versus "progressive" in the culture wars, for instance, or "conservative" versus "liberal" or "modernist" in theological matters. But we are less conscious of this automatic polarizing tendency in our own hearts and minds and of its severe consequences. In 1853 an observer noted the widespread impression "that an intellectual clergyman is deficient in piety, and that an eminently pious minister is deficient in intellect."[9]

The same is not only common today, but its roots have grown worse. The resulting polarization is now far deeper than many realize. The conflict is not just between different theological conclusions but between entirely different ways of thinking about everything—one shaped by high culture and the other by popular culture. Are there practical consequences of this polarizing tendency? Of course. All ideas have consequences. Tellingly, the first college-educated graduate of Francis Asbury's Indiana circuit riders found such hostility to his education that he gave up the regular ministry. But who could argue with Asbury's vision? Faced with a parish the size of continental Europe (excluding Russia), his vision for the Methodist circuit riders was heroic. And he never asked his preachers to endure what he himself did not endure. Asbury averaged five thousand miles of riding each year for three decades. He never found time to marry, build a home, or accumulate more possessions than a horse could carry.

"Studies" versus "the Loss of one Soul"? A learned ministry versus a living ministry? John Wesley, the founder of Methodism, had said, "It is a fundamental principle with us that to renounce reason is to renounce religion, that religion and reason go hand in hand, that all irrational religion is false religion."[10] But to such a heroic band of later Methodists, that choice was no choice. The life of the city pastor living like a gentleman was not for them. Poor, single, ill-paid, self-educated, and worn out they may have been, but they were on fire. Thousands of them had little education, scores had no education at all, but their zeal more than made up for it. Studies were a luxury they could not afford and did not need. The mold of evangelical anti-intellectualism was shaped for solid reasons.

Since that time different variants of polarization have emerged. Some have been more brazen—for example, Billy Sunday's brash philistinism: "If I had a million dollars, I'd give $999,999 to the church and $1 to education."[11] Or William Jennings Bryan, "If we have to give up either religion or education, we should give up education."[12] Others have been milder—such as today's campus polarizations mentioned earlier. Others still have been widely justified but deadly—such as the only-in-America notion that it is legitimate to separate an acceptance of

Christic as Savior from an acceptance of Christ as Lord (a sorry case of testimony overruling theology). All reveal a critical, two-hundred-year flaw in the evangelical mind. As Charles Malik warned in his address at the Billy Graham Center, "The problem is not only to win souls but to save minds. If you win the whole world and lose the mind of the world, you will soon discover you have not won the world. Indeed it may turn out you have actually lost the world."[13]

Until this flaw is addressed, the antagonisms are overcome, and evangelicals hold to a vision of Christian truth that displays wholeness and integration, evangelical thinking can be faithful neither to the lordship of Christ nor to the intellectual challenges of today's world.

2

PIETISM

THE SECOND INFLUENCE THAT HELPED TO UNDERMINE what was left of the Puritan mind and leave its mark on evangelicalism is pietism. Unlike a polarized view of truth, which is always and utterly wrong, pietism in itself is neither wrong nor destructive. On the contrary, its concerns are the very heart concerns of the Christian faith. On balance its influence is gloriously positive—without it, for example, there would have been no modern missionary movement or Great Awakenings.

Pietism is a "heart religion," an understanding and way of believing that places piety, or total life devotion, at the center of the Christian faith. Long a feature of Christian orthodoxy, pietism became a recognizable religious movement at the end of the seventeenth century. As such it stands as a movement of revival in protest against other emphases, such as sacramentalism and doctrinalism, and other tendencies, such as ritualism, legalism and—most importantly—intellectualism.

Whenever the spiritual ground is dry, pietism has been the main fruit of the "mighty rain" that refreshed it. In giving this primary place to total life devotion to God, the pietist seeks to obey the imperatives of the Old and New Testaments directly. Loving God and living life with a love for God at its heart are the essence of both the Jewish and Christian faiths.

A SPIRITUALITY FOR THE SIDELINES

Like any brand of faith, however, pietism has been corrupted and distorted at times. Some of the worst forms of distortion have occurred outside the English-speaking world and have no direct bearing on the rise of American anti-intellectualism. But they help us see the potential for distortion. Dietrich Bonhoeffer, for example, was a confirmed foe of the corrupted German pietism of the 1930s. With its emphasis on devotion foundering in the shallow waters of religious sentiment, Protestant pietism promoted the myth of the "dear God" who spreads his cloak of sentimental love over everything.

Distorting Luther's doctrine of the two kingdoms, pietists emphasized the sphere of inwardness, personal bliss, and private salvation—and therefore could raise no altar strong enough to resist the challenge of Adolf Hitler. Article 2 of the Barmen Declaration in May 1934 almost echoed Kuyper in its strong stand against the weakness of pietism and the dangers of National Socialism: "We reject the false doctrine that there are areas of our life in which we do not belong to Jesus Christ, but to other lords."

Because of what Bonhoeffer saw as its fundamental deficiency, he was relentless toward pietism. He believed it was a last-ditch attempt to preserve Protestantism as a religion, an instrument for the self-actualization of those who had been squeezed out of the centers of cultural power. With all else gone, pietists still had their "stop-gap God" in a little spiritual niche on the sidelines of the world. Their exposure of the inward sphere was shameless, a sort of religious striptease to suggest deep, intimate experiences with God, which they had never had. Pietists, Bonhoeffer concluded, had become an "escapist church," a community of "salvation-egotists" that was no longer the salt of the earth and the light of the world.[1]

Dietrich Bonhoeffer's reaction to pietism was unquestionably rooted in the personal. As a Prussian and an aristocrat, he did not believe in talking his faith to death. He abhorred the shameless religious clichés and the quick and easy manner of reporting conversion experiences. He never tired of calling attention to the fact that the Jews never uttered the name of God. Whatever the roots, his charges against the Protestant pietism of his day are largely accurate. They illustrate the sorry degeneration of a once vital spiritual and theological movement. The story of the corrupting of German pietism is a useful reminder to us today. Modern evangelical pietism in America has not degenerated that far. But the outline of the same weaknesses has emerged—especially in the form of a stop-gap, privatized faith that, in one observer's words, is "socially irrelevant even if privately engaging."[2] The emergence of anti-intellectualism two hundred years ago is central to the story of this degeneration of American pietism.

THE GREAT EVANGELICAL MELTDOWN

True orthodoxy, I must stress again, has piety at its heart. Anti-intellectualism was not a feature of the original pietism but only of a degenerating pietism. Thus when Philip Jacob Spener, the "father of pietism," founded Halle University in Germany, it was a mecca of pietism known for its strong integration of worship, learning, and social justice. Similarly in the United States, the First Great Awakening led to the founding of some of America's most eminent colleges and universities—such as Princeton, Brown, Rutgers, and Dartmouth.

But such acts and institutions soon became sidebars to the main story as evangelicals were caught up in the flush of an anti-intellectual pietism, especially in the Second Great Awakening in the early nineteenth century. As this happened, pietism itself was deformed. Reinforced by the polarization discussed earlier, the core themes of the Puritan mind shifted or disappeared—from the objective to the subjective, from the covenantal and communal to the individual, from election to voluntarism, from Calvinism to Arminianism, from the liturgical to the informal, and from a stress on theology to a stress on experience. Above all, the urgent question, "How do I know I am saved?" was increasingly answered in purely subjective terms—either as "Have you decided to be saved?" or "Have you gone through the experience of being saved?" Those who are reformed in their theology and thinking today must not be superior about this shift to Arminianism. The shift was an express repudiation of the Calvinism of its day—and with good reason. One nineteenth-century observer described the preaching heard in the Presbyterian pulpit before the Second Great Awakening as "a dry, speculative orthodoxy, leaving the heart without interest, and the conscience without alarm."[3]

Similarly, Joseph Haroutunian, a theologian of reformed background, gave a penetrating critique of the collapse of reformed thinking in the generation after Jonathan Edwards.

> The profound tragedy of Edwards' theology was transformed into a farce by his would-be disciples, who used his language and ignored his piety. . . . The logic of Calvinistic piety was being transformed into a vast, complicated, and colorless theological structure, bewildering to its friends and ridiculous to its enemies. It was like a proud and beggared king, hiding his shame with scarlet rags and yellow trinkets.[4]

The change was as if American evangelicalism, suddenly freed geographically from New England and theologically from Puritanism, experienced a massive meltdown of the core of the Puritan, Christian, or biblical mind. Doubtless anti-intellectualism was an overspill and unintended consequence of success. Evangelicalism was on a dramatic path of growth. It was as free, fluid, and fiery as the frontier required.

The same was true in the South. Bishop Benjamin T. Tanner of the African Methodist Episcopal Church described which methods really worked.

> While the good Presbyterian parson was writing his discourses, rounding off the sentences, the Methodist itinerant had traveled forty miles with his horse and saddle bags; while the parson was adjusting his spectacles to read his manuscript, the itinerant

had given hell and damnation to his unrepentant hearers; while the disciple of Calvin was waiting to have his church completed, the disciple of Wesley took to the woods and made them re-echo with the voice of free grace. . . .[5]

The trouble was that after the movement of revivalistic pietism swept by, evangelicalism had also become anti-intellectual and anti-theological to a fault. Examples of this anti-theological anti-intellectualism abound. "My theology!" Dwight L. Moody said later, "I didn't know I had any."[6] "If I had a creed," Sam Jones, the Moody of the South, added, "I would sell it to a museum."[7] Billy Sunday did not "know any more about theology," he used to boast, "than a jack-rabbit knew about ping pong."[8]

Faith without theology? Creeds fit only for a museum? Theology at a jack-rabbit level something to brag about? The statements themselves are flamboyantly brash; the assumptions behind them appalling. But they reveal our evangelical anti-intellectualism beyond any contradiction.

Current versions of anti-intellectual pietism are milder and sometimes even a little uneasy. But they have not been forsworn. And again and again our pietist flaw shows through. Whenever evangelicals have an experience of direct, personal access to God, we are tempted to think or act as if we can dispense with doctrine, sacraments, history, and all the other "superfluous paraphernalia" of the church—and make our experience the sum and soul of our faith.

Thus our evangelical experience has become our strength and our weakness. We are people with a true, sometimes a deep, experience of God. But we are no longer people of truth. Only rarely are we serious about theology at a popular level. We are still suspicious of thinking and scholarship. We are still attracted to movements that replace thinking and theology by other emphases—relational, therapeutic, charismatic, and managerial (as in church growth). Some of our ministries and organizations that operate at the highest levels of national life are still deeply, explicitly, and persistently anti-intellectual.

Whatever the other virtues of these movements and the unquestionable importance of piety, we must courageously repudiate anti-intellectualism for the sin it is. Piety is essential, but it is not sufficient by itself. Truth, thinking, theology, and the place of the mind must be given the emphasis they deserve from followers of Christ.

3

PRIMITIVISM

THE THIRD INFLUENCE THAT HELPED TO UNDERMINE what was left of the Puritan mind and leave its mark on evangelicalism is primitivism. Like pietism, primitivism has many aspects that are positive; what needs watching are the negative consequences of its overspill. But unlike pietism, primitivism requires more explanation. As we shall see, its consequences are easy to understand. But what it is and where it came from is more obscure.

Primitivism, sometimes called restorationism or restitutionism, is the impulse to restore the primitive or original order of life as revealed in the Scriptures. It has been a powerful theme in America's history, especially one important root and one important flowering in the evangelical movement. A defining feature of many great religions and civilizations is their special sense of time, particularly their sense of their "first" or primordial times and their "last" or millennial times. Some stress one, some the other, some both. Both the classical Chinese and Roman Empires, for example, put their emphasis on the "first times" and therefore on the "ancients" and the "ancestors."

THE LAND OF NEW BEGINNINGS

Where does the United States stand in terms of its view of time? Many people automatically respond in terms of our fascination with the future. But this is only half the story. The themes and

40

myths of American history are as rich with references to the past and "first times" as to the future and "last times." American impulses and rhetoric are as much about restoration as progress. The United States, Ronald Reagan said as he quoted Tom Paine, once more had the power "to begin the world over again."[1] From the early Puritan colonists to the later frontier settlers, America has been the land of new beginnings, second chances, and fresh opportunities. The earliest times have always had a powerful hold over American minds.

The virgin freshness of the American continent and the sheer novelty of the American experience are a prime source of primitivism. Another source is the Enlightenment, with its view that ordering things according to reason restored things to their place in the original natural order. "We are brought at once," Tom Paine wrote, "to the point of seeing government begin, as if we had lived in the beginning of time."[2]

For evangelicals a third source of primitivism is critical— the Reformation. The whole thrust of the Puritans and evangelicals was the Protestant impulse to reach back continually to the purity of the New Testament church. As John Cotton declared in his sermon before John Winthrop and his fearless four hundred on the Southampton dockside in 1630, the new commonwealth must be in harmony with "the first Plantation of the Primitive Church."[3] He affirmed that the New England way was as close as could be to what "the Lord Jesus [would erect] were he here himselfe in person."[4]

Historians have argued over the wider consequences of the primitivist impulse. Sometimes, they say, primitivism served a positive function, like a beacon of light from the past to illuminate and judge the present. But sometimes its effects are seen as more negative. When a nation or group within a nation identified itself with the purity of the first times it was liable to fall prey to the illusion of its own innocence. It therefore would be blind to its own shortcomings. Primitivism, in short, is an ingredient of American hypocrisy.

SIMPLE BUT NOT SIMPLISTIC

What matters here is the impact of primitivism on evangelical thinking. There have been two main legacies. First, the impulse of primitivism has contributed to the evangelical bias toward the simplistic. Because the primitive is the pure, the original, and the desirable by definition, all that is developed, settled, and institutionalized is obviously questionable. American evangelicals therefore characteristically display an impatience with the difficult, an intolerance of complexity, and a poor appreciation of the long-term and disciplined. Correspondingly we often demonstrate a tendency toward the simplistic, especially in the form of slogans or overly simple either/or solutions.

Second, primitivism has contributed to the evangelical bias against history. Because beginnings are always pure and a return is always possible by definition, the intervening history is seen as a matter of corruption and decline. We create the illusion that we can easily build anew and escape history and historical forces at will.

For Alexis de Tocqueville this American sense of history-lessness is closely tied to the excessive individualism in democracy. "The woof of time is every instant broken," he wrote, "and the back of generations effaced. Those who went before are soon forgotten; of those who come after, no one has any idea. . . . Thus not only does democracy make every man forget his ancestors, but it hides his descendants and separates his contemporaries from him; it throws him back forever upon himself alone and threatens in the end to confine him entirely within the solitude of his own heart."[5]

Today primitivism as a conscious impulse has weakened drastically. The seventeenth-century Puritans wanted to reestablish the "primitive" or "ancient" order in their congregational life. (Roger Williams's life—punctuated by leaving church after church—was one long quest for "the first pattern" of God's church.[6]) The eighteenth-century Methodists reached back for John Wesley's ideal of restoring the apostolic faith. The nineteenth-century Churches of Christ worked for a "restoration of the Ancient Order of Things." But twentieth-century evangelicals seem to hunger for little more than a vague but contentious "Christian America."

Although the impulse is weak at a conscious level, the overspill from its earlier, stronger days is still strong. Evangelicals must surmount our two-hundred-year-old bias against history and slant toward the simplistic. For our age is both rootless and complex. The former requires a sense of history and the latter some sophistication. Without these we can be neither effective nor faithful.

4

⁓⁓⁓⁓

POPULISM

THE FOURTH INFLUENCE THAT HELPED TO UNDERMINE what was left of the Puritan mind and leave its mark on evangelicalism is populism. Understood as a movement committed to the rights, wisdom, and virtues of common people, populism is one of the greatest strengths and weaknesses of both evangelicalism and America as a whole. Populism is therefore double-edged like pietism and primitivism. Its assets are strong and undeniable, but so also are its liabilities, which we must not overlook.

The origins of evangelical and American populism lie in the period between 1780 and 1830. As Nathan Hatch has described in his classic study *The Democratization of American Christianity*, this period was one of the most chaotic, original, and decisive periods not only in American but modern history. The American Revolution triggered a massive crisis of cultural authority from which came a dramatic shift—from the ideas and concerns of the Enlightenment and classical republicanism to those of democracy and grass-roots individualism.

At its heart, democratic populism was born of two influences: a passion for revival as in the First Great Awakening and a passion for popular sovereignty as in the American Revolution. Hatch describes the result as a form of populist religion of the people, for the people, and by the people. This in turn helped shape three characteristic features of American history—the vitality of mass democratic movements, the centrality of religion among ordinary people, and the prominence of populist religious leaders in both religious and democratic movements.

FAITH AND FRONTIER

Hatch argues that the significance of populism for the United States and the Christian church is incalculable. Populism simultaneously "democratized Christians" and "Christianized America."[1] It maximized faith's popular effect, in contrast to faith's irrelevance to the working classes in Europe. At the same time, it minimized popular opposition to faith, in contrast to the dangerous alienation of working people in Europe. Most importantly too, populism meant that "faith" and "frontier" joined together as the two explosive impulses of democratic expansion in nineteenth-century America.

The impact of populism on American religion was revolutionary. As Hatch notes, the genius of the American church since then has not been its ecclesiastical organization, the credibility of its apologetic, or the prestige of its clergy and leadership. It has been the strength of its anti-elitist, anti-centralist appeal in popular culture.

Once again populist religion, like pietism, was ideally suited to the period of frontier expansion. For example, a Congregational pastor, Horace Bushnell, commented on the admirable fit between Methodism and the frontier conditions. The Methodists, he said, were superbly adapted to the new West. They were "a kind of light artillery that God has organized to pursue and overtake the fugitives that flee into the wilderness from his presence."[2]

THE MAGNA CARTA OF THE COMMON MAN

The legacy of anti-intellectualism grows directly from the common characteristics of populist religion—unpretentious leaders, self-evident doctrines, lively music, vernacular communication, and locally run churches. Early nineteenth-century populism, it must be stressed, was never totally anti-intellectual. Even where it was, it was never anti-biblical—just as many types of twentieth-century fundamentalism are much less anti-intellectual than much soft-minded, middle-class evangelicalism.

But once again what matters is the unintended consequences of populism. The strengths of populism became its weaknesses. The same factors that constituted the positive side of populism also conspired to make it opposed to history, structure, organization, tradition, class, hierarchy, education, and even doctrine. By denying the distinction between clergy and laity, populism refused to defer to theology or theological training. By rejecting traditional learning and showing scant regard for canons of orthodoxy, populism tended to take all ideas and experiences at their face level. This opened the floodgates for heresy and newly created religions.

Above all, populism rejected educated leadership and put a boundless trust in the common person. The result was a populist style of interpretation in which the right to personal judgment became "the Magna Carta of the Common Man." Under the rallying cry "No creed but the Bible," each man or woman became his or her own interpreter.

Out of all the intensity and vitality of populism there were three contributions to anti-intellectualism. First, populism contributed to naïveté. Again and again populist religious leaders were so emphatic about what they had rejected—Calvinist theology and their clerical status above all—that they mistakenly thought they were free of all philosophical frameworks and any historical shaping of their faith and thinking. In reality, of course, they had only swapped one system of thought for another. They were more shaped by their culture than they realized.

Elias Smith, a New England pastor who abandoned his Calvinism and his ministerial calling at the same time, naively announced: "Having lost all my system, my mind was prepared to search the Scriptures." Similarly, Alexander Campbell, founder of the "Disciples of Christ," declared: "I have endeavored to read the Scriptures as though no one had read them before me, and I am as much on my guard against reading them today, through the medium of my own views yesterday, or a week ago, as I am against being influenced by any foreign name, authority, or system whatever."[3] Lewis Sperry Chafer, the founder of Dallas Theological Seminary, wrote in the same vein later: "The very fact that I did not study a prescribed course in theology made it possible for me to approach the subject with an unprejudiced mind and to be concerned only with what the Bible actually teaches."[4]

Second, populism contributed to an excessive leveling in the churches. As such, it became a form of democracy run riot. The same Elias Smith, for example, repeatedly attacked such churches as the Baptists and Methodists and called his followers simply "Christians." "Let us be Republicans indeed!" he cried, "Many are republicans as the government, and yet are but half republicans, being in matters of religion still bound to a catechism, creed, covenant, a superstitious priest. Venture to be as independent in things of religion, as in those which respect the government in which you live."[5]

Third, populism contributed to evangelicals' lack of respect for theology and a disengagement from serious discussion of truth. As historians point out, the real struggle in the period 1780–1830 was not between evangelicals and deists but between those who took theology seriously and those who did not. In 1808, for example, Andover Seminary was founded as an alternative to Harvard College because of the deepening apostasy of the latter. Yet as Hatch notes, in his inaugural sermon Timothy Dwight, president of Yale College and grandson of Jonathan Edwards, did not attack deism but populism.

Dwight's assault was on those "who declare, both in their language and conduct, that the desk ought to be yielded up to the occupancy of Ignorance. While they demand a seven-year apprenticeship, for the purpose of learning to make a shoe, or an axe, they suppose the system of Providence, together with the numerous, and frequently abstruse, doctrines and precepts, contained in the Scriptures, may all be comprehended without learning, labor, or time."[6]

This old theme has not faded away. It can be heard, for instance, in the megachurch dismissal of seminary training for pastors. I quoted John Schaar earlier about America being a predominantly Protestant nation with more Protestant believers than any other Protestant nation. But this nation has had almost no great native Protestant thinkers and theologians since Jonathan Edwards. Populism is the principal reason why. As the Pentecostal leader A. J. Tomlinson claimed, "We have the Bible for everything, and we have no creeds, rituals, or articles of faith."[7]

In the face of such nonsense in our heritage, our task is plain. We evangelicals must assess our populist heritage realistically and take a more discerning stand against its liabilities. Otherwise we will perpetuate its limitations, fatally handicap ourselves in a world of experts and elites that is not congenial to populism, and never enter into the profundity of the simple faith that is ours.

5

PLURALISM

THE FIFTH INFLUENCE THAT HELPED TO UNDERMINE what was left
of the Puritan mind and leave its mark on evangelicalism is pluralism. Here the relationship to anti-intellectualism is not what
many evangelicals may think. Pluralism's influence on evangelicalism has been as direct and damaging as many people fear.
But it did not happen either at the time or in the way that many
imagine.

THE "P WORD"

In the last generation many evangelicals have become gripped by
a phobia over pluralism. A tenacious axiom has formed that pluralism is a dangerous evil associated automatically with relativism. Small and innocuous-sounding at first, the confusion
between pluralism and relativism has enormous consequences
for evangelical thinking and public witness in an increasingly
pluralistic age.

There is a definite link between pluralism and relativism
that is part philosophical and part psychological. Such books as
Allan Bloom's *The Closing of the American Mind* drew attention
to it and its accompanying dangers, such as indifference to truth
and error, right and wrong. But to equate pluralism and relativism is as harmful as divorcing the two. It muddies the clear
thinking necessary to combat the real problem. A number of

considerations will help evangelicals rethink the issue and avoid the perils of this confusion.

First, philosophically speaking, pluralism is not in itself relativism and need not entail it. There is, to be sure, a technical philosophical doctrine of pluralism (whose opposite is the philosophical doctrine of monism) that includes a belief in the relativity of all truth. One modern proponent of this position was Bertrand Russell, who described his position as "logical atomism" or "absolute pluralism." But as used almost universally today, the term pluralism refers to a social reality, not a philosophical doctrine.

Pluralism is a social condition in which numerous different religious, ethnic, and cultural groups live together in one nation under one government. Pluralism, in this sense, is a social fact and not, like relativism, a philosophical conclusion. Pluralism is thus the end product of a process—technically known as "pluralization"—that is at the heart of modernity and modernization. "All those others" of different faiths happen to be in almost every part of the world today, and no amount of seeing red over relativism will wish them away.

Second, historically speaking, the past provides an antidote to, rather than a warrant for, the "P word" phobia that grips some evangelicals when public policy issues touch on pluralism. For one thing, evangelicals should appreciate the close link between religious liberty and pluralism. From the seventeenth-century Middle Colonies on, increasing diversity has presented both a contribution and a challenge to religious liberty. Religious liberty makes pluralism more likely; pluralism makes religious liberty more necessary.

Further, we evangelicals should trace our long and mostly fruitful relationship to pluralism in our own history. Was it not the highly pluralistic setting of the first century A.D. in which the number of early Christians grew explosively without compromise to their exclusive allegiance? Was it not the Protestant principle of freedom of conscience that contributed decisively to religious liberty and became the greatest generator of choice and dissent in history? Did not nineteenth-century evangelicalism show itself ready and able to exploit the "free market" opportunities for enterprising faiths that were opened up by the First Amendment's separation of church and state?

Third, culturally speaking, pluralism today tends to reinforce particularism—a belief in the importance and distinctiveness of particular faiths—just as much as relativism. Seen from an international perspective, such forces as nationalism, tribalism, and fundamentalism are a stubborn feature of the modern world. Seen from an American viewpoint, the sixties-style first response of pluralism-as-relativism (typified in education by values clarification theory) is giving way to the present position of pluralism-as-particularism.

The shift in popular metaphors of America being a melting pot to a mosaic, salad bowl, patchwork quilt, or kaleidoscope illustrates a deeper shift. As minorities have grown and diversity has widened, an appreciation of differences has deepened. Differences are seen to make a difference. Thus a stubborn feature of contemporary pluralism is the high number of people who are anything but relativists. These people, whether Christians, Jews, Mormons, Muslims, humanists, or atheists, unrepentantly believe their convictions to be absolutely true. In the end, this is even attested by the fact that "everything is relative has become the last absolute"—the relativist's own absolute. Even Sigmund Freud, the relativizers' relativizer, expressed his own beliefs dogmatically: "We possess the truth. I am sure of it."[1]

Fourth, politically speaking, pluralism may turn out to be the last, best hope for tradition rather than its inevitable destroyer. As Peter Berger points out, and the Central and Eastern European revolution of 1989 underscored, capitalism, pluralism, and freedom go hand in hand. Capitalism—unlike socialism or totalitarianism—leaves room for the development and maintenance of a multiplicity of ideas, institutions, and ways of life. Traditional institutions are included in this free, or relatively free, space. Berger's conclusion thus overturns expectations of the average conservative:

Capitalism means pluralism. Tradition has a better chance to survive under pluralism than under an integrative collectivism. . . . Capitalism is a thoroughly modern phenomenon, perhaps even the most modern phenomenon of all. But capitalism also relativizes modernity and imposes constraints on the modernization process. And, given a modern world that cannot be wished away, capitalism proves the best chance for non-modern beliefs and institutions to survive in this world.[2]

RELATIVISM BEFORE SECULARISM

The full story of the relationship of pluralism and evangelicalism is not all positive, of course. But we can understand it best if we distinguish it clearly from the current phobia over the "P word." Pluralism's contributions to anti-intellectualism cannot be blamed on the malevolence of contemporary secularism. The fact is that evangelicalism was pulled toward relativism by the tidal force of pluralism long before secularism became a vital force in American society.

Pluralism made two important contributions to evangelical anti-intellectualism. First, pluralism helped to create what John Murray Cuddihy has called "a religion of civility."[3] True civility is very positive. It is a style of public discourse and engagement shaped by a principled respect for people, truth, the common good, and the constitutional tradition. As such, it is a civilized prerequisite for knowing how to live with our deepest differences.

But the "religion of civility" is different. It is a corrupt form of civility—an oppressive form of tolerance—that in seeking to give no offense to others ends with no convictions of its own. This pseudocivility, or intolerant tolerance, begins with a bland exterior of permissive ecumenism—everybody is welcomed—but ends with a deep-rooted relativism hostile to all serious differences and distinctions. "Tolerance," G. K. Chesterton said, "is the virtue of those who don't believe anything." Or as Ronald Knox, another Catholic apologist, wryly observed, "Comparative religion makes people comparatively religious."

Yet here is the sting. Many evangelicals object rightly to modern forms of intolerant tolerance that become a patronizing form of discrimination and control. But what they often forget is that the stronger early forms of it were Protestant. A Roman Catholic priest in Detroit described Protestants to Alexis de Tocqueville as *rienistes,* or "nothingarians," because of their affable tolerance of all shades of conviction. Tocqueville himself wrote in a letter to a friend in 1831, "This so-called tolerance, which, in my opinion, is nothing but a huge indifference, is pushed so far that in pubic establishments like prisons . . . seven or eight ministers of different sects come to prison successively to the same inmates."[4]

DEEDS, NOT CREEDS

Pluralism made a second negative contribution to evangelical anti-intellectualism. It reinforced Protestant indifference to truth by shifting the accent from belief to behavior—or in the nineteenth-century maxim that has become an all-American truism, "Deeds, not creeds."

The reason for this lay in the practical dynamics of pluralism. In the struggle to compete, characteristic of the laissez-faire market of American religions, the tendency was to put forward one's best foot—and most attractive beliefs. Thus the focus was on the universal and the appealing, not on the particularistic or the divisive. The result, not unnaturally, favored good behavior at the expense of right beliefs. As Tocqueville noted about Protestantism, "Go into the churches, you will hear morality preached, of dogma not a word."[5]

This old tendency is the reason why, in historian Martin E. Marty's description, America is religiously speaking a "nation of behavers" rather than believers. Truth is commonly regarded as divisive, clarity of distinctions is not prized, and serious thinking is reckoned unnecessary. One irony is often pointed out: "heresy," which is clearly defined and arguably a matter of eternal consequence, has become less important to the average American

Protestant than "un-American," a concept defined nowhere and unarguably of lesser importance to the believer. The implications for anti-intellectualism are obvious. Modern evangelical thinking is riddled with relativism. But only a part can be blamed on secularism and the secularity of the modern world. The deeper, older part—rooted in a bland tolerance that holds no convictions and an esteem for good behavior over sound doctrine—is our responsibility alone. Until we clearly understand pluralism and root out all traces of indifference to truth, the scandal and the sin of anti-intellectualism will only grow worse in our pluralistic age.

6

PRAGMATISM

THE SIXTH INFLUENCE THAT HELPED TO UNDERMINE what was left of the Puritan mind and leave its mark on evangelicalism is pragmatism. What matters here is the subtlety of pragmatism's similarity to faith. Just as pietism has become synonymous with the Christian faith for evangelicals, so pragmatism is synonymous with the American way of doing things. Pragmatism is therefore self-evident to most Americans. It is so entirely taken for granted that few people bother to take account of either its assets or liabilities. Pragmatism, many seem to believe, is all gains and no losses.

PRAGMATISTS BEFORE PRAGMATISM

William James, the Harvard philosopher and psychologist of religion, founded the formal philosophy of pragmatism. Working at the end of the nineteenth century, he held that religious beliefs were only true because of their consequences for human behavior, not because of their philosophical claims. Truth, in other words, was not an absolute. It was an attribute that beliefs acquired as they were worked out in practice.

James's immediate influence was not on evangelicalism but on Protestant liberalism—through the practical relativism that was the hallmark of his thinking. But evangelicals were not immune to pragmatism. The truth is that evangelicals were pragmatists long before James. They were pragmatists well before pragmatism was a self-conscious philosophy. The reason lies in the American experience. Just to be American was to be "ex-European." The chief meaning of early America was liberation from Europe and a repudiation of the past. The Promised Land of the New World provided a refuge from the tyranny, luxury, decadence, and irreligion of the Egyptian fleshpots of the Old.

A key part of this required national reaction was to ideas in general and theology in particular. To be American was not only to be "ex-European" but to be opposed to European " 'isms and 'ologies." After all, Americans knew well that such 'isms and 'ologies were dangerously divisive in the Old World and useless in the New. American conditions, by contrast, had no place for unnecessary sophistication, let alone bickering over ideas. What mattered was hard work, common sense, ingenuity, and know-how. This was true both in the Frontier era when the American continent was won and in the later Age of Business when its resources were developed.

In short, American experience put a premium on pragmatism. The result was twofold: a characteristic evangelical pragmatism that became pronounced by the end of the Second Great Awakening and the explosion of Jacksonian populism that has been part and parcel of American evangelicalism ever since.

PAUL APPEALING, PEALE APPALLING

The influence of pragmatism on evangelicalism can be traced in several different places. One flamboyant outgrowth, which predates the early nineteenth century, was the rise of the prosperity doctrines or the "health and wealth gospel." The early Puritans, in contrast, had a striking combination of "diligence" in worldly business yet "deadness" to the world. All success, including wealth and fame, was therefore "dead works" to the believers as they pursued their calling. All that mattered was faith, for what puffs up someone in prosperity will make them murmur in adversity—unbelief.

There was a great shift, however, between the early seventeenth-century Puritans, such as John Cotton, and the mid-eighteenth-century Puritans, such as Cotton Mather. Coming just a generation after Mather, the philosophy of Benjamin Franklin shows how drastic the shift had been. Born in the closing days of the Puritan world, Franklin became an American success-prophet who turned the Puritan ethic upside down. "Doing well" by "doing good" became an American tradition. In the new piety of prosperity, individual salvation was now *through* good works. And industry, above all other virtues, was the road to prosperity. Christian behavior therefore had immense utilitarian value. Christian theology was less important—what mattered was that it worked, not that it was true.

A second outgrowth of pragmatism is the long stream of "self-help" and "positive thinking"—the general belief that optimistic thinking carries beneficial results. The sources contributing to this characteristically American school of thought run far wider than the churches. Immigrant experience, for example, reinforced the universal hope for a better life. Similarly, the tributaries of positive thinking flowed out far wider than the Christian faith. Different expressions of positive thinking can be heard in Ralph Waldo Emerson's transcendentalism, Mary Baker Eddy's Christian Science, and William James's "religion of healthy-mindedness."

But positive thinking has deeply affected evangelicalism too. Historians trace optimistic pragmatism right back to the First and Second Great Awakenings. During this time Arminianism superseded Calvinistic theology. People openly stressed encouraging human effort to transform the human will. Through human effort, then, others would accept the free offer of salvation. Gradually religion itself was changed. Instead of being a revelation by which we are criticized, it becomes a power to which we are adjusted for the sake of gaining our own power—and thus the key to health, wealth, popularity, and peace of mind. Thus the note of "spiritual technology," later picked up by the New Age movement, was introduced first by evangelicals. As one writer put it, "God is a twenty-four-hour station. All you need to do is to plug in."[1]

Twentieth-century versions are well known, supremely Norman Vincent Peale's 1952 best-seller *The Power of Positive Thinking* and Robert Schuller's television ministry "The Hour of Power." ("There is enough power in *you*," Peale wrote, "to blow the city of New York to rubble."[2]) The former occasioned Adlai Stevenson's celebrated quip: "Paul I find appealing, but Peale I find appalling."

THE ENGINEERING OF REVIVAL

Mention of the shift from Calvinism to Arminianism during the Second Great Awakening leads to the third outgrowth of pragmatism—its expression in mission and evangelism. Here the key figure was Charles Grandison Finney, "the father of modern revivalism." Under his preaching in the "burned-over district" of Western New York, a series of revivals broke out in the mid-1820s. At their heart was Finney's use of "new measures"—a series of innovations that included the use of the anxious seat (the sinner's bench), deliberately protracted meetings, special music, allowing women to pray in public, exerting direct pressure on individuals—sometimes by name—and so on.

Finney's methods were not original. He borrowed them from the Methodists. But because of his success he was highly criticized by supporters of the "old measures." On the one hand, his new methods accented the human initiative instead of the divine. On the other hand, they gave rise to a sense of "engineered" or "worked up" revival. Revival could occur whenever Christians used the proper means. As Finney argued forthrightly about revival, "It is not a miracle, or dependent on a miracle in any sense. It is a purely philosophical result of the right use of the constituted means—as much so as any other effect produced by the application of means."[3]

Finney's methods have been a defining feature of evangelicalism ever since. They have been demonstrated by later evangelists, such as D. L. Moody and Billy Sunday, or by the evangelistic approaches of the 1940s and 1950s. Billy Sunday, for instance, boasted to his sponsors that if "Gipsy" Smith could win converts for $4.92 apiece, he could cut the cost to $2.00 a soul when he got his system working.

Reliance on methods has even been lifted to new heights by the church-growth movement. From parking-lot theory to platform-dress style, everything in worship as well as evangelism can now be engineered and enhanced. Like a Disney theme park, many a megachurch has a fussbudget management system that dictates how employees must dress, talk, smile, and groom themselves.[4] Through it all pragmatism has become part of the evangelical soul. Finney's "right use of the appropriate means" is our hallmark. Though often decrying the culture of our times, we evangelicals characteristically view technology as neutral and use it uncritically to advance the gospel.

The overall result of such different trends as prosperity piety, positive thinking, engineered revivalism, and the church-growth movement has been to stamp pragmatism indelibly on the evangelical soul. The concern "Will it work?" has long overshadowed "Is it true?" Theology has given way to technique. Know-whom has faded before know-how. Serving God has subtly been deformed into servicing the self. At its worst, the result is a shift from faith to the "faith in faith," which—along with faith in religion—is a perniciously distinctive American heresy. But even at its best, pragmatism results in an evangelicalism rich in ingenuity and organization but poor in spirituality and superficial, if not banal, in doctrine. We have become the worldliest Christians in America.

Our challenge as evangelicals today is to weigh the assets and liabilities of pragmatism and see where we can correct the disadvantages while conserving the advantages. Once again both the gospel and our times demand no less.

7

⌘

PHILISTINISM

THE SEVENTH INFLUENCE THAT HELPED TO UNDERMINE what was left of the Puritan mind and leave its mark on evangelicalism is philistinism. The word Philistine originally described a native of Philistia. This was the ancient region of Canaan whose inhabitants the Israelites dispossessed as they entered the Promised Land. Over time, however, because of the barbarian status of the Philistine giant Goliath whom David killed, "Philistine" came to be a pejorative term. It described someone who was either crucially uninformed in a special area of knowledge or openly disdainful of intellectual or artistic values.

Needless to say, the pejorative use of the word can be dangerous. It can easily be used to mask the arrogance of a particular intellectual or of the cultural elite, thus providing a rationalization for their disdain for common people. After all, they suggest with a superior air, the "masses" simply cannot understand. The great "unwashed public" is irredeemably "uncultured and Philistine." We, by contrast, "the elite minority" the "vanguard of the mind and spirit," are different and superior.

But one extreme does not excuse another. The charge of philistinism can be a justifiable accusation even if a snob levels it. And in the case of evangelicalism, the primary evidence comes from us—not them.

Put differently, evangelical philistinism results from the impact of the previous six influences cast in a reactionary mold.

When evangelicals gloried in the simplistic and reacted to the sophisticated, when evangelicals stuck to the traditional in a hidebound way and protested the very mention of change, when evangelicals identified with the rural over against the urban—using the populist perspective against the elite—and when evangelicals later dug in their heels defending the fundamentals against the modernists, the result has been a powerful tendency toward philistinism.

REAL MEN DON'T NEED THEOLOGY

Billy Sunday lived and worked well after the pre-Civil War era we are examining. But he is probably the epitome of the evangelical "philistine." Known as "the baseball evangelist," he received little formal education. So when he left his major league baseball career to pursue itinerant evangelism his philistinism was part of his enormous appeal to ordinary people. Along with his down-home language, flamboyant antics, theatrical poses, and impassioned gestures, his backwoods philistinism put him squarely on the side of the general public and against its leaders.

Always in favor of the "one-hundred percenter," Jesus "the scrapper," and militant masculinity, Sunday cried typically, "Lord save us from off-handed, flabby-cheeked, brittle-boned, weak-kneed, thin-skinned, pliable, plastic, spineless, effeminate, ossi-fied, 3-carat Christianity."[1]

Millions heard Billy Sunday and hundreds of thousands came to faith in Christ at his meetings. He is also credited with helping to pass the Prohibitionist Amendment and with helping raise millions of dollars on behalf of World War I. But his brazen philistinism, along with his blatant appeal to toughness and his use of ridicule, also helped to cast in concrete the anti-intellectualism that had emerged in evangelicalism a generation earlier. "When the word of God says one thing," Sunday cried, "and scholarship says another, scholarship can go to hell."[2]

There were, of course, more moderate expressions of philistinism too. Wheaton College is noted today for its superb scholarship in many fields, including literature—as well as for its far-sighted interest in such great twentieth-century Christian writers as C. S. Lewis. But Jonathan Blanchard, Wheaton's first president in 1860, is well-known for such pronouncements as: A novel is "a well-told lie."[3]

Behind such anti-cultural and un-Christian statements lie a deficiency in theology. As evangelical pietism steadily narrowed its focus until it concentrated on the issues of salvation at the expense of those of creation, it lost its capacity for thinking Christianly—let alone thinking about culture and the arts. If a Jonathan Blanchard is more moderate and earlier than a Billy Sunday, there are expressions of philistinism at the heart of the Jacksonian era too—supremely Charles Grandison Finney.

Classically educated and trained at Yale College though he was, Finney displayed his own strain of philistinism. "I cannot believe," he once declared, "that a person who has ever known the love of God can relish a secular novel. . . . Let me visit your chamber, your parlor, or wherever you keep your books. What is here? Byron, Scott, Shakespeare and a host of triflers and blasphemers of God."[4]

Such philistinism has cast a long shadow in evangelicalism. On the one hand, it reinforces the prejudice that hides behind populist disdain for those such as "the media elite." On the other hand, it blocks evangelicals from truly appreciating culture and the arts. It also isolates evangelical artists—and poets, scriptwriters, sculptors, dancers, and actors—as the least understood and most alienated single group of people in the evangelical churches.

We live in a day when much of both highbrow and lowbrow culture is a grand assault on the Christian gospel. Sustaining the Philistine strand in our anti-intellectualism is therefore doubly wrong. Nowhere are the scandal and the sin more foolish.

8

PREMILLENIALISM

THE EIGHTH INFLUENCE THAT HELPED TO UNDERMINE what was left of the Puritan mind and leave its mark on evangelicalism is premillenialism, especially in its dispensationalist form. Premillenialism is the only influence of the eight that clearly came after the Civil War—it became popular among American evangelicals in the 1870s. But its influence was harmful later precisely because of how it converged with the other seven influences to produce a mindset that has often been openly hostile to thinking Christianly about life and culture.

Premillenialism itself is not the problem. Sometimes called chiliasm, it is the belief that the present age of human history will end in Christ's thousand-year reign on earth. This teaching is based on the first ten verses of Revelation 20, understood in light of Old Testament prophecies of a coming period of messianic justice and peace on earth. Prominent among premillenialist beliefs is the conviction that the thousand-year reign of Christ will be heralded by a series of signs marking the arrival of "the end times"—such as the preaching of the gospel to all the nations, wars, famines, apostasy, and the appearance of the anti-Christ.

Premillenialism, I stress once more, is not itself the problem. Many passionate premillenialists have also been passionately committed to loving God with their minds—the apologist Francis Schaeffer, for example. Dispensational premillenialism, however, has had unfortunate consequences on the Christian mind. Dispensationalism is the belief that all time and history can be divided into distinguishable periods, or dispensations, through which God deals with human beings in different ways. Each dispensation is a new time of testing for human beings that ends in judgment. Thus each dispensation represents the complete failure of human enterprise.

The idea of dividing history into periods is not new for Christians, but dispensational premillenialism is the most detailed and comprehensive system of its kind. It originated in the 1820s in Ireland from the teaching of John Nelson Darby (or JND), who broke away from the Church of Ireland and founded the Plymouth Brethren. As the Brethren movement expanded Darby visited the United States and Canada seven times between 1859 and 1874. His strong separatism in relation to the institutional church and his equally strong pessimism about the direction of modern society did not find wide acceptance in North America. But his fresh view of the systematic unfolding of prophetic events—which soon became known as dispensationalism—attracted many leaders of late nineteenth-century evangelicalism, such as Dwight L. Moody and A. J. Gordon.

Dispensationalism later became a powerful movement through four main avenues—the Bible conference movement, Bible colleges, the Scofield Reference Bible (published in 1909), and the rise of the Dallas Theological Seminary under Lewis Sperry Chafer (founded in 1924). C. I. Scofield, who identified seven distinct dispensations, soon replaced Darby as the canonical authority of American dispensationalism. Many conservatives rejected his formulation at first. But as the movement spread, Scofield's became the standard version of dispensationalism just as dispensationalism became the dominant version of premillenialism. Today dispensational premillenialism is a defining feature of fundamentalism and much of evangelicalism. It is typified for many people by such runaway best-selling books as Hal Lindsey's *The Late Great Planet Earth*.

CASTING THE DIE

Needless to say there is extraordinary diversity within the dispensationalist movement. There are also great differences between responsible scholarship at one end and careless but bestselling speculations at the other end. And there are differences between earlier, more flamboyant dispensationalists and more recent and careful "progressive" dispensationalists. Perhaps surprisingly to many people, its roots were heavily Calvinist. All comments and criticisms therefore require careful qualification. But most agree that dispensationalism has adversely impacted the earlier Christian mind in a number of ways.

First, the dispensationalist movement reinforced the antiintellectualism of the seven earlier trends. Far from setting out to counter them, it actually reinforced them. This occurred at a time when evangelicals urgently needed to counter the late nineteenth-century secularization of education. Populism, for example, finds enthusiastic support in both the teaching and style of dispensationalism. If once-powerful churches and denominations are rotting from apostasy, if in these "end times" decadence is spreading through civilization and secularism through its leaders, if both the church and the world are beyond reform and beyond hope this side of the millennium, then the only answer is simple, basic, biblical truth taught by simple, basic, biblical believers.

Properly understood the logic is impeccable. Did not Jesus himself, they say, speak with "a note of authority" rather than "notes and authorities"? And so it is easy to see how dogmatic populism flourishes in such a climate. Not only the newly secularizing universities and colleges of the late nineteenth century but all formal learning is suspect. What is always prized, by contrast, is charismatic certainty. For when biblical infallibility blends into personal infallibility and becomes dogmatic certitude, the way is open for self-styled and self-assured populism of the worst sort.

A recurring feature of dispensational populism is its careless crossover between the Bible and historical events of its day. At its worst, the result is what Francis Schaeffer—a premillenialist himself—called the "This is that" fallacy. This fallacy is to think that "this event in our time is the fulfillment of that prophecy in the Bible." Every generation and speaker, for example, points to its own proof-texted-beyond-any-doubt anti-Christ. In my lifetime they have included people as diverse as Adolf Hitler, Henry Kissinger, and Saddam Hussein.

But, of course, when "this" does not turn out to be "that," few people openly say that the speaker or writer was wrong. Those who see the contradiction often claim that the Bible was wrong. Those who do not see it have usually followed the speaker to a newly identified anti-Christ and have no ears for anything but the new focus of alarm. Considering our evangelical genius for technological innovation, I was surprised that it was the generally other-worldly Lubavitcher Hasidic Jews who first set up a toll-free Messiah hotline and first carried beepers so that they could be reached at once with news of the Messiah's arrival.

In the 1990s milder versions of dispensational alarmism surround such topics as the New World Order. Forget that the world's localizing and fragmenting forces are as strong as the globalizing and integrating forces—so that "Little worlders" are as much in evidence as "One worlders." Forget that "order" within the American tradition is not a centralizing process but a federalizing one that promotes diversity within the bounds of unity—in John F. Kennedy's phrase, "making the world safe for diversity." Dispensational populism dances skillfully between biblical themes, modern trends, and human fears. It comes out with a red-meat rhetoric of alarm that is as wildly successful as it is wrong-headed and irresponsible.

A FIREFIGHTER'S THEOLOGY

Second, the dispensational movement reinforces anti-intellectualism by its general indifference to serious engagement with culture. Put simply, it is a form of the earlier false polarization and shrunken pietism reinforced by a distracting preoccupation

with the end times. The roots of the problem, as ever, are theological. Dispensationalists at the popular level tend to overlook
creation as they emphasize salvation, the lordship of Christ for
the cross, common grace for special grace, the visible present for
the invisible future, and the normal and everyday for the dramatic and the apocalyptic.

Little wonder that popular dispensationalism has cultural
consequences. When the house is on fire, life is worth more than
books and precious objects. When the end times are on the slip-
way, such cultural pursuits as art and music are frivolous. Where
earlier Christians fell into dualism by placing the spiritual above
the secular, contemplation above action, "full-time Christian
service" above ordinary life, and "soul saving" above study, many
dispensationalists have followed the course of "end times" events
with the consuming fascination of a betting man at a race track.
In doing so they have virtually turned their backs on the world in
which they live.

Third, the dispensational movement has often had overlooked unintended consequences. By reinforcing anti-intellectualism, evangelicals became vulnerable to various habits of
thinking that originated in the nineteenth century rather than
the Bible. Put simply, dispensationalism called evangelicals to
"flee the world," but did so in a way that laid them open to new
forms of worldliness. This irony has been pointed out by such
historians as George Marsden and Mark A. Noll and such
theologians as Thomas C. Oden.

The main example here is the characteristic dispensationalist
reliance on the capacities of a supposed objective, neutral,
detached, and impartial science that the nineteenth century
favored. This supposition from both a biblical as well as a contemporary viewpoint amounts to naïveté. Other intellectual
habits of the nineteenth-century world—which unsurprisingly
are both worldly and transient—include a neglect of the forces of
history that shape an age and an extreme dismissal of tradition
and the wisdom of previous ages. As Mark Noll concludes, "In
these terms, the problem of fundamentalism was that the worst

features of the nineteenth century intellectual situation became the methodological keystones for mental activity in the twentieth century."[1]

Noll's observation could be applied not only to dispensational premillenialism but to all the other seven influences—polarization, pietism, primitivism, populism, pluralism, pragmatism, and philistinism. Once these influences raged like a fire through the evangelical movement, what remained of the earlier Puritan mind was devastated, a ghost mind was created, and evangelical thinking was vulnerable to the ravaging pressures of mass culture in the twentieth century. It is this to which we turn next.

PART
TWO

AN IDIOT CULTURE

IN 1994 A HIGH SCHOOL SENIOR sent Georgetown University an application for admission with a shoe. As he had one foot in the door, he joked, how about letting in the other? Similarly the University of Michigan received an essay in a three-dimensional format with 3-D glasses attached; Harvard University was sent an application written by foot; Bowdoin College got a poem etched on bark; Wheaton College, Massachusetts, was flooded with watercolors, sculptures, slides of artwork, and cookies in the shapes of animals; and the University of Maryland had a glut of applicants sending "obituaries" that mentioned their years in College Park.

Gone are the days, it appears, when students can simply rely on the excellence and originality of their writing. The competition of ideas and expression has given way to a game of gimmicks in which originality has become zanyness. The result, says the president of the United States Students Association, is the "I am different, you want me" phenomenon. This has joined grade inflation as part of the idiocy of current American education. At Stanford University, for example, less than 10 percent of the students receive anything below a B grade.[1]

Now before anyone tut-tuts with disapproval we must acknowledge the passionate defenders of such new approaches. Japanese leaders, such defenders argue, lament that the United States is declining into a second-rate power with young people suffering from laziness and illiteracy. But the fact is, the defenders continue, that young Americans are more creative and better prepared for the future than their critics realize. All those years of watching television screens, devouring computer graphics, and manipulating Nintendo knobs and buttons have trained them surprisingly well for the new age.

Such dead white male authors as Mark Twain and James Joyce may now be off the screens of American students' computers. But in a world of visual literacy, information saturation, consumer savvy, and hi-tech wizardry, the whole idea of cultural education has changed. Young Americans are far ahead of the curve, it is claimed. Why should anyone read Nathaniel Hawthorne and listen to William Shakespeare when modern life rewards a studious devotion to comic books, interactive technology, and MTV?

Needless to say, such cultural barbarianism has more attackers than defenders. Most Christians would range themselves solidly on the side of the concerned. Most of us would agree, for example, with recurring laments about "the dumbing-down of America" or with journalist Carl Bernstein's well-aimed diatribe against the creation of an "idiot culture." For two decades, Bernstein argues, we have moved

> toward the creation of a sleazoid info-tainment culture in which the lines between Oprah and Phil and Geraldo and Diane and even Ted, between the *New York Post* and *Newsday*, are too often indistinguishable. In this new culture of journalistic titillation, we teach our readers and our viewers that the trivial is significant, that the lurid and the loopy are more important than real news. We do not serve our readers and viewers, we pander to them.

In short, Bernstein concludes, we are creating the idiot culture. "For the first time in our history the weird and the stupid and the coarse are becoming our cultural norm, even our cultural ideal.[2]

At the same time, many Christians fail to realize how much the same "dumbing-down" process has affected us. For example, I never cease to be amazed how many questions at Christian meetings in America pivot on references to "the bottom line" or how many answers are requested "in twenty-five words or fewer." But more importantly still, many Christians also overlook how much this contemporary conformism to a "dumbed-down" or "idiot culture" completes the collapse of the Christian mind begun two hundred years earlier.

In Part One we examined the first phase of the story—the retreat from a Christian mind and the creation of a ghost mind. This process of hollowing-out was completed mostly before the Civil War. In Part Two we will look at the second phase of the story—the rise of a mass mind and the creation of an idiot culture. This process of dumbing-down is still being completed in our time.

TOO HIGHBROW BY HALF

Behind this analysis of Christian thinking deformed by an "idiot culture" are two important facts—the grand general fact of the rise of modernity (which I have analyzed elsewhere[3]) and a particular factor within it, a fork in the road that separates highbrow and lowbrow Christian thinking. Put differently, there have been two divergent trends in the world of knowledge since the Civil War. On the one hand, in terms of the content of knowledge—what is known—the trend has been toward specialization. On the other hand, in terms of the channels of knowledge—how it is communicated—the trend has been toward universalization.

Obviously our concern here is the second trend, the shaping of the Christian mind at the popular rather than the elite level. (Mark Noll's *The Scandal of the Evangelical Mind* provides a superb survey of the problem at the level of higher education.) Together the two trends form a pincer-like grip strangling what used to be a characteristic feature of American society—the "high average" of ordinary thinking under the conditions of democracy.

Many common people in the eighteenth and nineteenth centuries had a knowledge of Shakespeare and the Bible that people today would view as the preserve of the literary scholar or theologian. There simply was no literary aristocracy. By 1772, Jacob Duché could write, "The poorest laborer upon the shores of the Delaware thinks himself entitled to deliver his sentiment on matters of religion or politics with as much freedom as the gentleman or scholar. . . . Such is the prevailing taste for books of every kind, that almost every man is a reader."[4] But this old high average has gone. Because of the universalizing trend, today's everyday knowledge at the popular level is far below the old high average; because of the specializing trend, today's elite knowledge is far above the old high average.

George Steiner describes the result of modern mass education as "semi-literacy."[5] The ability to read is widespread, but the inability to read any but the shallowest texts is equally widespread. He cites recent estimates that put the literacy of more than half the population of the United States at the level of twelve-year-olds. Steiner concludes: "Such semi- or sub-literacy is not being eradicated by mass-schooling: it is being made politically and psychologically acceptable."[6]

Our focusing on the problems at the popular level does not mean that the elite level has no problems. Nor does it mean that the elite level holds any easy answers for the problems at the popular level. In fact the very divergence between the two is itself a major problem for the contemporary Christian mind. For it represents a severe dysfunction in the organic unity of the church seen as the "body" of Christ. With the Christian highbrow higher and more abstruse and irrelevant than ever and the Christian lowbrow lower and more vulgar and adolescent than ever, the body of Christ often gives the appearance of the uncontrolled movements of a paraplegic.

To be sure, there are no fixed boundaries between highbrow and lowbrow, elite culture and popular culture. The word "highbrow" only entered the English language in the 1880s, signifying a person of superior intellectual attainment. But it also carried a pejorative hint of conscious superiority to lower human standards—as in Matthew Arnold's "the clique of the cultivated and learned." The more colloquial term "lowbrow" followed a few decades later, signifying someone who is not or does not claim to be highly educated or refined. The rarer term "middlebrow" only followed in the 1930s. It is mostly used disparagingly of a style of thought capable of a higher way yet which reduces things to a lower way in the end.

This century-old war between the "brows"—high, middle, and low—bears on our story for one main reason. Christian thinkers who have taken the high road mostly disqualify themselves from helping out on the low road because of two things: their secularization and their specialization.

The first of these highbrow problems—secularization—is more obvious. It has both been documented carefully by such historians as George Marsden and Mark Noll and kept alive more accusingly by ordinary believers' suspicions of betrayal. So the story of the secularizing of Christian thinking is no secret. Following the Civil War, America went through a massive reorganization of higher education that effectually displaced evangelicals from their previous role as the intellectual arbiters of the nation. With the expansion of education, the exploding number of new students, the increase of graduate studies, the shift in profile of administrations, donors, and trustees, and the decline of the British model of education in favor of the German, a whole new concept of the university rose to replace traditional Christian higher education.

As Mark Noll concludes, the old synthesis of evangelical convictions, American ideals, and a commonsense science faded rapidly in the face of these changes.

> The collapse of that synthesis signaled the collapse of the effort by conservative evangelicals to construct a Christian mind in America. . . . The quality of Christian thinking may not have been high in antebellum America. But at least it was there. With the rise of the new university, evangelical thinking,

which had previously existed in the tension between academic and populist styles, became almost exclusively populist.[7]

The secularization of Christian thought ushered in by these climactic changes in the late nineteenth century was accelerated even further by a similar explosion of higher education following the Second World War. This was when the expansion of graduate studies and the research universities coincided with the GI Bill, the rise of the New Class, and the emergence of the "education gap" in American religion (discussed earlier).

But here the second snag in the highbrow approach becomes apparent too: Elite Christian thinking has not only become too secularized but too specialized. The resulting specialization and professionalization of knowledge creates a world where only other specialists can understand specialized knowledge. Expert knowledge therefore comes to be pursued as an end in itself. A gap is created between experts and ordinary people—and people who are experts in one field are often ordinary people in the field next door. Worse still, Christian thinkers often become closer to the "cultured despisers" of the faith than to their fellow Christians. And worst of all, such specialization fosters a myth of expertise and professionalism that creates dependency and becomes disabling for anyone but the professional.

The point is surely clear. An analysis of the problems of popular Christian thinking must not be mistaken for the assertion that elite Christian thinking is any better than popular thinking. Modern Christian intellectuals pose the danger of hubris just as much as gnostic intellectuals did in the second century. As Irenaeus put it then, "it does not follow because men are endowed with greater and less degrees of intelligence, that they should therefore change the subject matter of the faith itself."[8] Our urgent need is for reformation at both the highbrow and lowbrow levels—including "a bridging of the brows" that allows deep truth to be intelligible and practicable to all God's people in a whole and healthy way.

What follows, then, is an outline of some of the pressures shaping the Christian mind in America at the popular level.

Needless to say, the list is only a sample, the treatment only brief, and the different pressures are closely related because they are all different facets of modernity (for example, the relationship between television, the triumph of the image, and the humiliation of the word, or between postmodernism and style).

For those who want to go further, many of the surveys focus on one book that can be used as a helpful, single volume introduction to the topic in question. But the following list throws light on the source and style of modern pressures that make our thinking more like the "idiot culture" around us than the mind of Christ within us.

9

AMUSING OURSELVES TO DEATH

AMERICA IS A COUNTRY WHERE "I read that book" has become an acceptable non-readers' euphemism for having heard of the title. And "I don't watch TV" has become the cryptic self-identification of readers who see themselves as an endangered species in tele-land.

Quite obviously no account of contemporary American thinking is complete without a mention of television's influence on reading and thinking. But here the very glut of studies, arguments, and personal opinions make fresh arguments almost superfluous. Probably the best single introduction to the issue, however, is Neil Postman's *Amusing Ourselves to Death*.[1] It captures both the essence of television and its impact on thinking and discourse.

American cities, Postman argues, have always been the focal point of the radiating American spirit—Boston in the eighteenth century, New York in the nineteenth century, and Chicago in the early twentieth century. Today, however, Las Vegas is the metaphor of American character and aspiration.

> For Las Vegas is a city entirely devoted to the idea of entertainment, and as such proclaims the spirit of a culture in which all public discourse increasingly takes the form of entertainment. . . . The result is that we are a people on the verge of amusing ourselves to death.[2]

76

THE AGE OF ENTERTAINMENT

Needless to say, Postman traces this problem not to the door of the Las Vegas Chamber of Commerce but to television. Television has contributed to the vast shift from an "age of exposition" based on typography to the "age of entertainment." From its beginning until well into the nineteenth century, American thinking and discourse was as dominated both by the printed word and by speech shaped by the printed word as any society in history. Seventeenth-century America was an extremely literate society. The founding of the United States in the eighteenth century was successfully led by intellectuals, which itself is a rare occurrence.

Certain assumptions and expectations were built into the age of exposition. They could be counted on effortlessly, whether by professors before their classes, pastors preaching to their congregations, or politicians addressing the electorate. In the age of exposition, speakers and writers could always assume a serious attention span, a remarkable comprehension level, considerable sophistication concerning the world and history, and a relatively rigorous style of argument. In short, American thinking and speech in the age shaped by the printed word were substantive and serious. Americans had something to say and a real purpose in saying it.

Television, Postman argues, is not the sole culprit in effecting the shift from the age of exposition to the age of entertainment. It is simply the single most powerful and persuasive medium in which the graphics revolution has culminated. But behind television lie two earlier inventions—the telegraph, which put the focus on the "instant," and the photograph, which put the focus on the "image." Television's real potency, therefore, is its blending of instancy and image. Television's real problem, however, is that through this blending entertainment becomes the master-style of television.

The problem, Postman stresses, is not that television has too much entertaining subject matter, but that all subject matter on television is presented as entertainment. "In courtrooms, classrooms, operating rooms, board rooms, churches, and even airplanes, Americans no longer talk to each other, they entertain each other. They do not exchange ideas; they exchange images. They do not argue with propositions; they argue with good looks, celebrities, and commercials."[3]

Again, the deepest problem is not the mindlessness of television but how television transforms even the life of the mind into entertainment. Biographer Ronald Steel, for example, compares two eminent journalists, Walter Lippmann from the early-twentieth century and George Will from today. Is the latter—with his yearly million-dollar income—a journalist, a paid performer, or a conglomerate? "Lippmann didn't have much use for either radio or television. He was an elucidator. Mr. Will is an entertainer."[4]

THE "NOW THIS . . ." WORLDVIEW

What matters for our purpose is television's influence on American discourse and therefore its pressure on the Christian mind. However much television we watch—from little or none to too much—it is now so omnipresent in society that its biases need continued vigilance.

First, television discourse has a bias against *understanding*. With its rapid images, its simplistic thought, and its intense emotions, television is devoid of the context needed for true understanding. Its superficiality amounts to a form of disinformation. "Disinformation does not mean false information. It means misleading information—misplaced, irrelevant, fragmented, or superficial information—information that creates the illusion of knowing something, but which in fact leads one away from knowing."[5]

Second, television discourse has a bias against *responsibility*. The same rapidity, variety, and intensity of images that provides the viewer no context for true understanding also prevents the viewer from engaging with the consequences of what is experienced. The abrupt—sometimes absurd—discontinuities between programming and advertising particularly makes this so. "There is no murder so brutal, no earthquake so devastating, no political burden so costly . . . that it cannot be erased from our minds by a newscaster saying, 'Now . . . this.' "[6]

Third, television discourse has a bias against *memory* and *history*. Its very pace and style create a nonstop preoccupation with the present. Incoherent perhaps, irresponsible certainly, the ceaseless, breathless flow of the Now renders viewers incapable of remembering. As television superjournalist Bill Moyers laments, "We Americans seem to know everything about the last twenty-four hours but very little of the past sixty centuries or the last sixty years."[7]

Fourth, television discourse has a bias against *rationality*. With rare exceptions, television so disdains "talking heads" that the very act of thinking becomes unthinkable on television. A thinker questioned might pause to reflect, "Now let me see . . . What do you mean?" But on television such thinking is too slow, too uncertain, too boring. As any aficionado of such shows as "The McLaughlin Group" knows, television answering is performing, not pondering. It is theatre rather than thinking, entertaining drama rather than edifying debate. To criticize such shows as if they were anything else is to miss the fun, they would say.

Fifth, television discourse has a bias against *truth* and *accuracy*. Credibility was once linked to veracity—someone or something was believable because of being true or not true. Today, however, credibility serves as a synonym for plausibility— whether someone or something seems to be true. Credibility in the television age has little to do with principle and all to do with plausibility and performance. "Is it true?" is overshadowed by "Was it compelling/sincere/entertaining/charismatic?" The smile and the assured answer now carry the day.

Critics of television have applied analyses like Postman's to many areas, including its influence on education, democracy, and even personal solitude. Italian film director Federico Fellini, for example, charged that "Television has mutilated our capacity for solitude. It has violated our most intimate, private, and secret dimension."[8]

Our concern here is with thinking alone, but that challenge is difficult enough. As Ted Koppel, host of ABC's *Nightline*, warned, "How does one explain or, perhaps more relevant, guard against the influence of an industry which is on the verge of becoming a hallucinogenic barrage of images, whose only grammar is pacing, whose principal theme is energy? We are losing our ability to manage ideas; to contemplate, to think."[9] The importance of the challenge for followers of Christ is inescapable.

10

PEOPLE OF PLENTY

"ADVERTISING," SAYS THE CYNIC, "is the art of getting people to buy what they don't need by describing it in ways they know are not true." Yet advertising is not only as inescapable as death and taxes, it is central to American life as in no other society. By the age of twenty, we are told, the average American has seen about eight hundred thousand advertisements on television alone—or about eight hundred a week. This does not include countless others seen and heard through radio, print, billboards, and other forms of advertising. THAT, AND MUCH, MUCH MORE AHEAD, RIGHT AFTER THIS, SO STAY WITH US . . . . "ULTRA SLIM-FAST™—GIVE US A WEEK, WE'LL TAKE OFF THE WEIGHT!"

We may lament that beer and fast food commercials are more familiar to children than nursery rhymes. We may worry that the all-invasiveness of advertising has far outlasted the threat of Soviet communism. But advertising is not going to disappear any time soon. Life in America is life in Adland. Vance Packard's "Hidden Persuaders" (advertisers) of three decades ago are a great deal less hidden and a great deal more persuasive today. NOW THIS . . . "NOTHING SMOOTHES YOUR WAY LIKE MILKY WAY.™"

In the modern world, advertising is a colossal, increasingly global, and ever more sophisticated industry. It dominates the food we eat, the clothes we wear, the cars we drive, the newspapers we read, the programs we watch, the vacations we choose,

81

the toys our children play with, and the politicians we elect. NOW THIS . . . "CRABTREE AND EVELYN™—IT'S NOT JUST A STORE. IT'S A SANCTUARY."

Today presidential appeals are interchangeable with Pepsi commercials. "Infomercials" and "advertorials" signal the suave smile of advertising and public relations behind even news columns and book publishing. Theme stories are proliferating—as well as tie-ins, cash-ins, credits, spin-offs, hard sell, soft sell, recognition opportunities, "cross promotions," "cause-related marketing," and of course a manic creativity in licensing anything and everything. As the *Washington Post* has concluded, "It's an ad, ad, ad, ad world" in America.[1] NOW THIS . . . "MOMMY, WOW! I'M A BIG KID NOW."—HUGGIES™ TRAINING PANTS WITH NEW, IMPROVED LEAK PROTECTION.

Oddly enough, most Christians have paid far less attention to the pressures of advertising than to television. Advertising, however, is a major part of television whose influence is just as strong and whose damage just as pervasive. But Christians still tend to judge a medium by its message rather than seeing the medium itself as the main message. Thus television is "obviously dangerous because of its sex and violence," but what could be blander and more innocuous than advertising? NOW THIS . . . "GET OUT OF THE OLD. GET INTO THE COLD—MILLER GENUINE DRAFT.™"

In fact the insidiousness of advertising is closely related to its invisibility. Advertising is simply too all-American to be questioned, too much a part of the background of life to be noticed. For most of its history America's potent blend of natural abundance has lent substance and splendor to its mythic status as a land of plenty. From the Icelandic sagas of "Leif the Lucky" down to the competing promises of today's politicians and televangelists, prosperity as providence has been a basic theme in America's understanding itself. NOW THIS. . . "MISTIC™ SPRING WATER—IT'S SO NATURAL, IT'S LIKE GOING NAKED."

Few things are more typically American than the reported assertion of Franklin D. Roosevelt that, if he could place one book in the hands of every Soviet citizen, he would choose a

Sears Roebuck catalog. As historian David Potter shows in *People of Plenty*, his superb examination of the issue, advertising is integral to this quintessential American theme.[2] NOW THIS . . . "CANON™—IMAGE IS EVERYTHING."

Modern advertising is another significant development of the late nineteenth century. At the end of the Civil War ads were only given a small place, costing small sums of money. Mostly prosaic and factual and more like our "want ads" now, they were published by retailers rather than producers. There was little reference to brands or labels. NOW THIS . . . "CHRYSLER™—THIS CHANGES EVERYTHING."

By the 1880s, however, sudden and spectacular changes appeared. Vast new amounts were being spent, the entire appearance was altered (black and white breaking out into color and tiny boxes exploding into large spreads), new brands, labels, and trademarks were sprouting, and the whole nature of the appeal was transformed. With the shift from the age of scarcity to the age of abundance, the challenge was not to couple supply and demand but to create demand. With supply outstripping demand on a massive scale for the first time in human history, advertising became an essential means to create demand artificially. NOW THIS . . . "LIPTON™—THIS AIN'T NO SIPPIN' TEA!"

VENI, VIDI, *VISA*

Advertising is integral to the vital social shift from America being a society of producers to becoming a society of consumers. In the process, Potter contends, advertising became a primary American institution. Thus advertising shapes and forms America's standards and lifestyles just as schools and universities shape learning, churches and synagogues shape faith, the Senate and the House of Representatives shape politics, and corporations shape business. NOW THIS . . . "DR. PEPPER™—YOU'RE A PART OF ME!"

But more than that, advertising now influences all the other primary institutions—witness presidential politics or the electronic church. And unlike the others, advertising is unique as a primary national institution with no moral purpose, no social responsibility, and no idealistic objectives. The other primary institutions may not live up to their ideals, but at least they have them. Similarly, individual advertisers may have strong ideals, but advertising itself does not. Its bottom line is only the bottom line. Its sole purpose is simply to stimulate consumption or the desire to consume. NOW THIS . . . "WHY ASK WHY? TRY BUD DRY.™"

Sociologists and others have traced the influence of advertising and the wider ethos of consumption in many areas—especially on work satisfaction, the hedonistic revolution, and the complete dominance of the consumption ethic in our time. As the superabundance of the late forties and fifties grew into the excess of the "money years"—the 1980s—high consumption was transformed from an excess into an ethos and ethic. "Veni, vidi, Visa" crowed the bumper sticker. Or as author Ted Morgan wrote approvingly earlier, "The Eastern bloc has Marxism, and Americans have shopping-center theory."[3] NOW THIS . . . "WHAT YOU WANT IS WHAT YOU GET AT MCDONALD'S™ TODAY."

The outcome is what Robert Bellah has called "market totalitarianism." Market forces are invading and colonizing most of human life, subjecting it to the constraints and criteria of money. The result is an encroaching "commodification" of everything, the reduction of the human to the economic, behavior to self-interest, wisdom to "cost-effectiveness," success to "productivity," society to "an arena for competitive individualism," public life to "the market place," and human beings to "consumers" and "maximizers." MUCH MORE RIGHT AFTER THIS . . . "MASTER-CARD™—IT'S MORE THAN A CREDIT CARD. IT'S SMART MONEY."

ALL YOU LOVE IS NEED

But what is advertising's impact on American thinking and discourse? First, advertising is biased toward a secular, materialistic, and amoral view of life. Needless to say, I am not saying that advertisements actually argue for a secular, materialist, or amoral view of life. Or even that individual advertising agents have a secular, materialistic, and amoral view of life. The creators of ads may well be deeply human, profoundly moral, and passionately spiritual. But these things have no real place in their ads—except as "hooks." The entire advertisement centers on the consumer and his or her needs and desires. As sociologist Tony Walter points out in a clever reversal of the Beatles's song, "All you love is need." NOW THIS . . . "I LOVE WHAT YOU DO FOR ME, TOYOTA!™"

Second, advertising is biased against the independent audience and thinker. Whereas readers once were the key to a magazine's fortunes prior to the age of advertising, advertisers now are. Seen this way, the subscriber is now secondary. In a sense, therefore, the advertiser "buys" the magazine for the purchaser and the price is a "qualifying fee" to prove that the subscriber is a bona fide consumer of what the advertiser wishes to sell. In any successful article or program, truth and substance are *that which sell*. NOW THIS . . . "L'ORÉAL™—MORE BEAUTIFUL BY DESIGN."

Feminist leader Gloria Steinem made much of the power of advertising over women's magazines in the first issue of the redesigned *Ms.*, in which the subscription price was significantly raised and no advertisements allowed. In the May 1990 issue of *Vogue*, she said, only 38 out of 319 pages were "non-ad or ad-related." In the May 1990 issue of *Elle*, the number was only 36 out of 326. In the April 1990 issue of *Redbook* the number was 44 out of 173 and in the March 13, 1990 issue of *Family Circle* the number was 33 out of 180. A similar point lies behind the objection to "infomercials" and "advertorials"—commercials that pretend to be news and advertisements that masquerade as editorials. NOW THIS . . . "THE PRUDENTIAL™—PEACE OF MIND. IT COMES WITH EVERY PIECE OF THE ROCK."

Third, advertising is biased against substantive content. In a world dominated by advertising, newspaper features, magazine articles, or television programs are no longer simply ends in themselves. They are also means to an end—selling. Along with everything else they have to catch attention, for behind the article or the program is the ad and behind the ad is the product. The serious reader or viewer cannot escape his or her status as a supplicant beholden to Budweiser or Burger King. Worse still, the seriousness of the article or program is often affected too. As one European critic said of American periodical writing in the 1950s, it "fixes the attention but does not engage the mind." NOW THIS . . . "FUJI™—A NEW WAY OF SEEING THINGS."

Fourth, advertising is biased against thinking and discernment. Walter Lippmann pointed this out early in the century in connection with the mass media. The general opinions of a large number of people are usually vague and very easily confused. Persuasion in the day of the "phantom public" therefore consists essentially in the use of symbols that assemble emotions after they have been detached from their ideas. At its heart the process is one of an intensification of feeling and a degrading of significance. In short, advertising works best when it magnifies symbols, intensifies emotions, and simplifies thought—thus bypassing discernment. NOW THIS . . . "CHEVROLET—THE HEART-BEAT OF AMERICA."

Fifth, advertising is biased against the advanced and the controversial because they do not appeal to advertising's special target, the mass audience. By definition special appeals exclude or antagonize people in a mass audience. This problem is somewhat softened by the recent shift from broadcasting to "narrow casting," but it still holds true generally. Because of this inherent drive for the greatest possible appeal to the widest possible audience, advertising is naturally drawn to the simple and naturally repelled by controversy. NOW THIS . . . "PERT PLUS™—GREAT HAIR. NO FUSS."

What would it be like to continue reading with the constant interruption of advertising? Have we grown more accustomed than we should to its illogic and intrusiveness? Why do we accept absurd customs, such as the fact that car salespeople shout at us? Are we moving toward a world where we will see advertisements on the walls of Congress for State of the Union audiences? Will states, as the *Washington Post* asks, one day use acronyms and logos—so that, for example, the State of New York becomes SONY, brought to you by you know who. . . ?

When evangelicals mimic the messages of Madison Avenue and the sassiness of MTV, our flair for crassness grows unsurpassed—for example, "Christian T-shirts" with such slogans as "THIS BLOOD'S FOR YOU," "HIS PAIN—YOUR GAIN," "GOD'S BODY-BUILDING GYM," and "TURN OR BURN."

But at a far deeper lever, those who reflect on advertising—its biases and influence on American thinking at large—will see how contrary the spirit of advertising is to the spirit of Christian communication. As David Potter concludes of America's admakers, their concern is not with "finding an audience to hear their message but rather with finding a message to hold their audience."[5] Nothing could better state the built-in limits of such buzzwords as "seeker friendly" and "audience-driven." Nothing better highlights the mutual challenges of advertising and the Christian faith.

11

ALL CONSUMING IMAGES

"WHAT A PIECE OF WORK IS A MAN," Shakespeare wrote—but the great bard did so before the day of the machine-constructed men, turned out on Nautilus-lathes in America's million and one gymnastic assembly lines. I watched one this week. With sweat glistening on his brow and a magazine on the reading rack in front of him, he pedaled his exercise bike with the devotion and concentration of a medieval monk at his prayers or a nineteenth-century worker in a different sort of sweatshop. A handsome hulk of a man, he was the very image of the beautifully honed males who confront us daily in advertisements, magazines, and films as icons of masculine style.

An hour or two a day, five times a week, like medieval monks visiting the stations of the cross, our Nautilus men move from machine to machine as they work on their abdomens, hips, buttocks, quadriceps, calves, backs, shoulders, chests, triceps, and biceps. From machine to machine, body part to body part, mirror to mirror, and weigh-in to weigh-in, they go at it with exact instructions and deliberate precision ("taut by experts"). They work on their bodies like a piece of art or, more accurately, like a piece of engineering ("state-of-the-art appearance enhancement technologies"). Their attention to their bodies is a perfect expression of modernity—a slavish and self-absorbed dedication to the middle-class style of precisely defined, powerfully engineered body machines that today we call masculine.

Of course, other styles press onto us from a thousand sides. At the opposite end from the Soloflexed or Nautilused male (which includes a good many females) is the willowy, impossibly slim, anorexic female. And in between is the androgynous, sexless boy-girl of the gender-uncertain age. But what links them all—and not just images of the body but images of everything in American life—is style.

Style, style, style—style is a leading currency in modern society, the river of life for American consumerism, the main artery of American identity and belonging. It is another vitally important pressure on thinking and discourse. My suggested introduction to this third pressure is Stuart Ewen's *All Consuming Images*.[1]

The connection between television and advertising is obvious and strong; the same is true of style. Television in general and television commercials in particular are two of the strongest purveyors of style in America. Style, however, has an importance of its own apart from these two pressures. Yet style, of course, is slippery and hard to define. The term itself derives from the Latin word for stylus or pen. It came to refer to the distinctive manner in which someone wrote and therefore signified the distinctive manner of expression used by anyone or anything. At its heart style is a term of identification, as substance is. But style and substance are in direct contrast. Substance is a matter of who or what someone or something is; style is the manner through which that distinctiveness is presented and perceived.

The term "style" has traditionally identified the leading characteristic or ruling taste of a period or school—in the sense that we refer to "Romanesque" and "Gothic" architecture or to "classical," "impressionist," and "cubist" art. Each new style is in some ways a break from the past and embodies a different way of seeing or doing things. But what matters in this usage is that style is viewed as the outer expression of the inner character of the period. The style, therefore, is as enduring as the period itself.

Style as Self-Advertising

Today, however, style has become an end in itself. No longer expressive of substance or inner character, style is all that matters now. No longer enduring, it is transient, changeable, and fashion-oriented. As a glance at any magazine rack will show, style is the number one mantra of late twentieth-century America. Used more often on magazine covers than even the word sex, style is a leading source of anxiety, hope, and fascination for millions. To be up-to-date and in touch with one's style is essential; to be out-of-date or out-of-touch is unforgivable. At a time when permanence of personality is as forlorn as permanence of place, change is the order of the day. Identity is now a matter of perception and presentation. And style is the art of skillfully presenting illusions as we walk down the corridor of images that make up modern society.

From the perspective of its purveyors, style is the official currency of marketing products. From the perspective of consumers, style is the leading idiom of the image of one's choice—the desired sense of projected meaning and belonging. Style, image, and consumption are foundational to modern identity and discourse. In a world of increasing anonymity where scrutiny by unknown others is our daily norm, style is a sort of armor for city life. Wear something and walk down the street and you don't just say, "I like this," you say, "I'm like this."

As Stuart Ewen shows, style is the sorcery that turns the banal necessities of our everyday world into an enchanted utopia of mouth-watering freedom. This is the illusory world where no conflicts grate and no needs are unmet. If modern society is a Vanity Fair of consumable styles, style itself is the ultimate in human self-advertising.

One of the first to recognize the novelty of style in the modern world was Oliver Wendell Holmes. Holmes's essays in 1859 on the invention of the photograph predicted the rise of the era of style. He saw that the photograph was "an image with a memory." Because of photography, the time was coming when "the image would become more important than the object itself, and would in fact make the object disposable."[2] Photography makes it possible to reproduce the disembodied appearance of things, thus creating a vast market of images. "Every conceivable object of Nature and Art will soon scale off its surface for us. Men will hunt all curious, beautiful, grand objects, as they hunt cattle in South America, for their skins and leave the carcasses as of little worth."[3]

The two most obvious applications are advertising and fashion. Walter Lippmann wrote in 1914 that a seductive panorama of images was being constructed above the American landscape. Psychologically speaking, images were pictures painted to promote the pleasure of possession.

> The eastern sky [is] ablaze with chewing gum, the northern with toothbrushes and underwear, the western with whiskey, and the southern with petticoats, the whole heavens . . . [are] brilliant with monstrously flirtatious women. . . .[4]

This process came to a climax in the world of fashion. America's High Priestess of style for much of the twentieth century was Diana Vreeland, editor of *Vogue* and upmarket forerunner for Madonna. Her motto was "FAKE IT. FAKE IT." "Never worry about facts," she said, "project an image to the public." The art of success is to create a world "as you feel it to be, as you wish it to be, as you wish it into being."[5]

But Vreeland's reign as empress of style is only an American, mass-market version of what began far earlier in aristocratic Europe. French *haute couture* is legendary but neither new nor accidental. Jean Baptiste Colbert, financial adviser to the "Sun King," Louis XIV, stated it simply: "With our taste, let us make war on Europe, and through fashion conquer the world."[6] His strategy was the forerunner of Christian Dior and Pierre Cardin just as they were of Ralph Lauren and Calvin Klein—the promotion of goods distinguished for their aura of aristocratic style.

How has America's mania for style and image affected thinking and discussion? The potential damage is obvious, centering on the revolution behind the predominance of style. Substance is unimportant, style is what counts. Permanence is obsolescent, ceaseless change alone endures. Creation and creators are beside the point, consumption is its own purpose. Essences are ignored, only surfaces matter. Faces are seen by the millions, voices are rarely heard—and then only with words that are accessories to images. The tried and the true are of no interest, only the novel and the new have allure. The meaning of things does not count, the style's concern is for the mining of surfaces—for their look, touch, sound, scent. Intrinsic character is nothing, exterior personality is everything. Who we *are* takes second place to who we can *become* and who we *appear* to be. We may not be comfortable in our own skins, but style is the umbilical cord between sales and the self we would like to become. And so on and so on.

THE TRIUMPH OF CHRISTIAN LITE

Among many applications to Christian thinking, three are salient. First, preoccupation with style reinforces the trend toward trendiness. If change and choice are the two absolutes in modern society, then we slip toward a state described by French critic Roland Barthes as "neomania." This is the cult of the-latest-is-the-greatest and the-newer-is-the-truer. The pursuit of relevance for its own sake quickly leads to superficiality, anxiety, burnout, and compromise.

Second, preoccupation with style undermines Christian speech of all kind. Christian speaking on both the individual and public levels was once the art of communicating the understanding of truth and ideas. Increasingly it has become a matter of performance and even of pretense—for example, the use of the "ghost-written sermon," an anti-evangelical contradiction in terms if ever there was one.

Surveys show that only eight percent of an American audience pays attention to the content of a speech, 42 percent to the speaker's appearance, and 50 percent to how the person speaks.[7] Style has overpowered substance. As one consultant puts it, "Animation is the greatest cosmetic in the world." Neither the unprepossessing Apostle Paul nor his content-packed, reformation-triggering letter to the Romans appear to stand much chance under these conditions.

Third, preoccupation with style is a major ingredient of the emptiness in modern culture. Thus it affects the drive to sex and violence, which is the prime compensation for emptiness in a culture that has only one sin left—boredom. The modern world that is crammed with images and frantic with changing styles is a hollow world, but is too dazzled to see it. As I have argued elsewhere, hollowness is the disintegrative disease of weightlessness brought on by our crisis of cultural authority.[8]

As Friedrich Nietzsche predicted, "it would seem for a time as if all things had become weightless."[9] Artificiality was once connected with city life—witness T. S. Eliot's "Unreal City" and "The Hollow Men." Now it has shifted from the cityscape to the image-scape. A corridor of images and a hall of mirrors are hardly the place to discover truth, substance, and that gravitas or weightiness that is the essence of the glory of God. The result is a form of the faith that is Christian Lite.

Unlike television and advertising, style is something many Christians are barely aware of. Always in the background and always changing, its real significance is that it destroys all significance. And in the process it profoundly assaults us too.

12

THE HUMILIATION
OF THE WORD

"WORDS HAVE GONE WILD," Henri Nouwen lamented in the early 1980s. "Recently I was driving through Los Angeles. Suddenly I had the strange sensation of driving through a huge dictionary. Wherever I looked there were words trying to keep my eyes from the road. They said, 'Use me, take me, buy me, drink me, eat me, smell me, touch me, kiss me, sleep with me.'"[1]

Nouwen is certainly right that modern life is a barrage of words. Newspapers, radios, televisions, billboards, flyers, bumper stickers, road signs, and a million and one everpresent announcements—we are surrounded, inundated, and assaulted by noisy words as experienced by no generation in history before us.

Nouwen is right too that words in a wordy world have lost their power. "Words, words, words . . . mere words"—their very multiplication has undermined our confidence in them. They no longer communicate, convey truth and understanding, create community, or provide the common ground on which people can meet and build society. Noisy but empty, words have a Babel capacity for confusion and division that is stronger than ever.

Nouwen is right above all that the deepest antidotes to our word-noisy world are solitude and silence. These two spiritual disciplines help us wean ourselves from addiction to the world and free ourselves to live unhindered before the face of God alone.

But all that granted, Christians who go further than Nouwen by rejecting the place of words in faith and join the Gadarene rush to embrace images are guilty of a monumental folly. What Jacques Ellul has written of as *The Humiliation of the Word*, which is the reverse side of the triumph of the image, is a defining feature of modernity. And it is a powerfully damaging pressure on the Christian mind.

THE TRIUMPH OF THE IMAGE

The triumph of the image (and therefore of signs and style) and the humiliation of the word are two sides of the same coin. Both go back to what Daniel Boorstin called "the graphics revolution" and Jacques Ellul described as the "greatest mutation known to humankind since the Stone Age."[2] By the late twentieth century both men regarded the revolution as successful and the mutation complete. Images now dominate words—the visual over the verbal, entertainment over exposition, and the artificial (including virtual reality) over the real and the natural.

As Ellul stressed, the triumph of the image under the conditions of modernity is not a matter of philosophy and choice but rather of technology and change of environment. Modernity is a universe of images. Of course the premodern world had images—sculptures and stained glass windows in churches, for example. But on the whole images were rare and often expensive. They were mostly associated either with the wealthy or with worship. And, needless to say, there were no reproductions, photographs, and almost no museums.

Today, by contrast, images blot out nature. The world of fields, hedges, woods, and rivers has been replaced by a paper jungle of photographs, reproductions, signs, billboards, bumper stickers, comic books, charts, diagrams, labels, logos, trademarks, advertisements, and so on. Like it or not, this paper jungle is our total environment, our omnipresent way of life, our daily visual diet. Put more accurately, it is the nonstop cultural bombardment that assaults us.

At first sight, this revolution appears successful beyond challenge. The only question is whether we should join it and make the shift from words to images or whether we should resist it and become word-using Neanderthals. The Neanderthal is what Marshall McLuhan called a POB: a "Print-Oriented Bastard." For most people, the answer is decided purely on age. As cultural critic Camille Paglia said in her celebrated dinner conversation with Neil Postman:

> I've found that most people born before World War II are turned off by the modern media. . . . I'm forty-three. I was born in 1947. And you graduated from college in 1953. I checked! I wanted to know, because I think this information is absolutely critical to how one views the mass media. I graduated from college in 1968. There are only fifteen years between us, but it's a critical fifteen years, an unbridgeable chasm in American culture.[3]

Many Christians have deserted their two-thousand-year commitment to words and have sided with the triumphant image. Not so much because of their birthdate, perhaps. They have turned to the image either because they have been unknowingly influenced by the general cultural tide or because of high-minded commitments to such notions as "seeker-friendly" and "audience-driven." The first say, "Isn't this the world we live in?" And the second say, "How else will we reach people in an image-dominated age?"

HEROES OF THE WORD

For those who are not fainthearts, it is encouraging to note how many champions of the word can be found outside the church of Christ. Isaac Asimov, for example—author of more than three hundred books and an avowed atheist—attacked the mythologies of the image head-on. "You may have heard the statement, 'One picture is worth a thousand words.' Don't you believe it."[4] Images may be more powerful on occasion—as when someone is illiterate—but in many cases the statement is nonsense. (Asimov's point is reminiscent of George Bernard Shaw's remark on seeing the glittering neon signs on Broadway: "It must be beautiful, if you can't read.")

"Consider, for instance, Hamlet's great soliloquy that begins with 'To be or not to be,' the poetic consideration of the pros and cons of suicide. It is 260 words long. Can you get across the essence of Hamlet's thought in a quarter of a picture—or, for that matter, in 260 pictures? Of course not."[5] As soon as we have to deal with emotions, ideas, and fancies, Asimov continues, only words will do. "Pictures will not do; they will never do. Television is fun to watch, but it is utterly and entirely dependent on the spoken and written word."[6]

Atheist though he was, Asimov's conclusion was more biblical than many Christians who reflect on the topic today. "There is a fundamental rule, then. In the beginning was the word (as the Gospel of John says in a different connection), and in the end will be the word. The word is immortal."[7]

The same witness to the primacy of the word can be heard strongly in the Jewish community. For them the word both reaches back to the first things of their faith and reaches forward as a requirement for freedom and democracy. The Jews did not create a culture of monuments, like the Romans, but rather a culture of words. The prophet, Rabbi David Wolpe writes, is "the quintessential Jewish hero, the hero of the moral word."[8] Similarly, George Steiner argues, the human being is "the language animal." Language and humanness imply and require each other. "Humanity and that miracle are, or have been hitherto, indivisible. Should language lose an appreciable measure of its dynamism, man will, in some radical way, be less man, less himself."[9]

But this stress on words is only because words are what we are. Created by a word-speaking God, human beings are word-speaking people. Unless words have meaning, everything becomes chaos. Unless words have power, everything becomes barren. In Hebrew, the ten commandments are "the ten words." For the Jews, the heroism of Moses is partly that of an instinctive man of action who was not "a man of words," but whom God transformed into "the man who learned to speak."[10]

Our Puritan forebears would have been at home with this view. For them words and the Word were linked. Perhaps the most literate people in the history of the world, they gained their ideas and shaped their tough-minded thinking from one chief source—the sermon. Historian Harry Stout of Yale University estimates that the average New Englander heard seven thousand sermons in a lifetime—about fifteen thousand hours of concentrated listening. There were no competing voices, he points out, so the sermon was an even more influential medium than television is today.

Such tough-mindedness about words is rare in Protestant circles today. Our piety is soft-minded, even sentimental. But our best writers on the subject have warned us clearly enough. "Anyone wishing to save humanity today," wrote Jacques Ellul, "must first of all save the word."[11] (A century ago Søren Kierkegaard noted the beginning of the process. The Christian faith had become so diluted that what was needed "was to win back the lost power and meaning of words."[12])

Study the Scriptures, Ellul argues, and we find that the primacy of the word is constant and complete. God is "He who is," the one who lives and speaks. The word is therefore the way God creates and how he deals with us. Made in his image, we are the word-speaking, word-answering creatures who live response-able between his first word of creation and his last word of judgment.

More importantly still, words are integral to the drama of revelation and salvation—in direct contrast to images and sight. The original unity of word and vision has been ruptured by sin, so now God is unapproachable by sight ("No man shall see me and live"). Sight is now always associated with sin and hearing with obedience. Sight is also expressly linked to idolatry.

Of course, the Bible is not anti-visual. Jesus is the Word made flesh. Word and vision are complementary and inseparable; words have power because they have pictures in them. Seeing is thoroughly proper—that is, when it is limited to that which can be shown. And hearing is never superior to sight. It is merely

sufficient and necessary at a time when we have no sight of God
without holiness.

SAVE THE WORD TO SAVE THE WORLD

No one who wrestles with this biblical heritage can be content
with our evangelical irresponsibility about words today. What
are some of the effects on the modern Christian mind?

First, our word-deficient culture is heavily biased toward
image-dominated expression and perception. "Seeing is believing. . . A picture is worth a thousand words. . . The camera does
not lie. . . Enough of words. . ." These modern truisms loyal to
the primacy of the image trip off our tongues as self-evident,
taken-for-granted Christian verities. Are images artificial? Ficti-
tious? Easily manipulated? Potentially idolatrous? Never mind.
We live in a world where images are reality in unarguable form.
So evangelicals have followed suit and abandoned their Reformed
heritage. At the highest levels this shift has opened the door to
the more pictorial theology of Eastern Orthodoxy. At the lower
levels it has welcomed in trash and what is worse still—idolatry.

The link between images and idolatry is critical. Camille
Paglia openly celebrates the triumph of the image as the return of
paganism and idolatry—"We are steeped in idolatry. The sacred
is everywhere. I don't see any secularism. We've returned to the
age of polytheism. It's a rebirth of the pagan gods."[13] But too
many evangelicals forget the biblical link between image, sin,
and idolatry. They do not realize how our image-dominant culture is both essentially religious and decisively harmful to Christian notions of truth and falsehood.

Second, our word-deficient culture is biased against understanding. With an increasing reliance on visual communication,
the trend is to appeal to the emotions rather than the understanding. Even in advertising itself, young though it is, the traditional copywriter is becoming a casualty. The concern is no
longer to show what a product can *do*, but to use emotional
imagery to show how a consumer can *feel* about it. This trend

is further reinforced by communications going global, for emotion translates more easily than reason.

Hearing and reading are slow, sequential, demanding, and analytical processes. They put a premium on truth, understanding, and judgment. Visual communication, by contrast, is faster, easier, more immediate, and more intuitive. But it is often so "obvious" that it bypasses critical thought. It moves by association, not analysis. Words are not authoritative but accessories. "Thinking" can very easily develop from emotion to emotion. The outcome can be a jarring blend of intense convictions and incoherent arguments that is anything but seasoned, spiritual wisdom.

Christians should be wary of images, ancient and modern. But iconoclasm and a general smashing of images is no response. One day, we confidently anticipate, there will be a long-desired reconciliation of word and image, truth and reality. But to bring forward that day prematurely is as false as to oppose word and image altogether. In the beginning was the Word and in the meantime there is the word.

As Jacques Ellul says in the closing words of his book, our remaining task is "the daily struggle to make the word resound, alone and unshackled. During the space of time that separates us from this final sight, may the word resound for human freedom and for God's truth."[14] Nothing is more important for the well-being of the Christian mind.

13

CANNIBALS OF POMO

Not long after the second Russian Revolution of 1989, I spent an evening with a courageous survivor of fifteen years of the Soviet gulag. Imprisoned for political dissidence, he had entered the prison camps as a Jew but while there became a Jewish believer in Jesus Christ. Like Aleksandr Solzhenitsyn a generation earlier, he was converted through the testimony of fellow prisoners who were courageous followers of Christ. Like the great writer, he too had every reason to say, "Bless you, prison."

Along with his growing faith, one of the things that sustained this Russian brother through the grim, grey years of his sentence was the memory of his son—four years old when he entered prison and nineteen when he was released. "You can appreciate what I felt," he said, "as I went to meet my son for the first time after so many years. I was particularly eager to share with him the meaning of my new faith that had sustained me throughout the terrible ordeal."

"So you can imagine my joy," he continued, "when I met my son, now a young man, and saw that he was wearing a cross around his neck. Clearly, I thought, he had found his own way to Christ.

"But I was cruelly disappointed. When we had greeted each other and caught up on many things, I asked him about his cross and what it meant to him. He dismissed me abruptly.

" 'Father,' he said, 'For my generation the cross is just a fashion statement.' "

The cross a fashion statement? History's ultimate symbol of subverted shame and dereliction, illuminated in the gulag darkness, now cloyed with a sugar-coating and a gilt-edge? Is this the ultimate in gallows humor, cynicism, condescension, or what? Not really. It is simply an everyday example of the devouring character of late twentieth-century popular postmodernism at its most banal—and insidious.

Seen one way, this example is mild and unexceptional. It is poignant only because of the way in which the pent-up longings of this Russian brother were dashed. After all, countless Christians have reduced the cross to a fashion statement by the careless way they have worn it. Since the late nineteenth century, when style and substance parted company, the style market has been rich in what used to be called "delight in the unreal"—a craze for using objects for something more or other than they really are.

Papier maché has long doubled as rosewood, painted tin as marble, plastic as alabaster, glass as jewels. But in the late nineteenth century, one observer noted,

> The sideboard boasts copper vessels, never used for cooking, and mighty pewter mugs out of which no one drinks. On the wall hang defiant swords, never crossed, and proud hunting trophies never won. . . . A magnificent Gutenberg Bible is discovered to be a work-box, and a carved cupboard an orchestrion. The butter knife is a Turkish dagger, the ashtray a Prussian helmet, the umbrella stand a knight in armor, and the thermometer, a pistol.[1]

These examples of Victorian whimsy pale beside the cultural cannibalism practiced today in the name of postmodernism (popularly known as PoMo). Take Madonna, "female icon" of the 1980s. She is the ultimate spin doctor to her own PR, the consummate orchestrator of her own controlled, ever-changing, ever-commercial images. Call her shameless, call her cheap, call her cynical, call her pornographic, call her sacrilegious, call her what you like. There is no limit to what she will say, do, wear, mock, promote, degrade—all to draw attention to herself and sell her soul along with her latest image and product. As with other supercelebrities, even her publicity gets publicity. Compared with Madonna's deliberate abuse of Christian symbols, the Russian's was the soul of sincerity. No wonder James Dobson described Time Warner's publishing of her book *Sex* as "the most outrageous single event that has occurred in my lifetime."[2] Appalling? Often. But aberration? No. Madonna as a High Priestess of PoMo is the epitome of a fifth modern influence that confronts us in America today—popular postmodernism, including its devouring attitude to truth, goodness, and beauty.

IF YOU DON'T GET IT, YOU DON'T GET IT

Few words are more confused and abused than "postmodern." So before we examine popular postmodernism we need to look briefly at a more complicated issue behind it—the disputed relationship between postmodernism, modernism, and modernity.

Some say that the meaning of postmodernism is muddied because its use has mushroomed. Others say that it is used more and more precisely because it means less and less. Either way it is rarely clear what it means—Is it a hip word for the trendy and novel? A grab-bag term for everything after the modern? A buzzword additive to give an educated sound to a second-rate thought (like the use of "gestalt" in the sixties and "paradigm" in the eighties)? Is it a philosophy, a school, a mood, a nostalgia, a reaction, a sales fashion? Postmodernism sometimes seems to be anything anyone wishes it to be. As the proponents of PoMo say, "If you don't get it, you don't get it."

Yet vague, slippery, and confusing though the term may be, postmodernism is too important to be discarded casually. For what it gropes to describe is central to the character of our time. "Postmodern," whatever it is, is a term reaching out to describe the outline of a vanishing "modern," whatever it is. Both terms are critical for followers of Christ who seek to act, think, and know the world in which we live.

What is clear is how the term postmodern crept into usage. First used in the 1930s, the current vogue for postmodern developed from a reaction against high modernism in art and literature in the sixties and in architecture and style during the seventies. It became common coinage in many fields in the eighties. What else is clear are the commonly cited examples of postmodernism, such as Philip Johnson's AT&T building in New York with its Chippendale-scroll top. Finally, the dramatic contrast perceived between "modernism" and "postmodernism" is clear. This contrast, however, is partly suspect. Much of the clarity of modernism emerges, not from self-professed modernists, but from the attack on modernism by proponents of postmodernism.

Modernism, as its postmodern critics see it, is equated with "the Enlightenment project" as it worked its way out in philosophy, art, literature, architecture, and a score of fields of human endeavor. "God is dead and man has come of age," modernists claimed in a stance that was characteristically humanist, secularist, and rationalist. Rejecting God and traditional supernatural explanations, modernists retained the sense of such universal, transcendental norms as truth, freedom, justice, equality, progress, and beauty. But they based them on such purely humanist foundations as reason, science, technology, and Western tradition. "Man-come-of-age" therefore exuded self-confidence. He (and she) was soaring in his reach and expectations and superior in his attitude to previous ages and other cultures.

The story of the tarnishing of this shiny optimism needs no recounting. Always philosophically unstable, modernism has been slowly undone by the events and studies of the twentieth century. Two world wars, numberless regional wars and conflicts, industrial and environmental pollution, and nuclear armaments have all cast a shadow on the accomplishments of science. Technology and technical reason have produced a world that many people find alienating and dehumanizing—whereas modernists spoke glowingly of houses as "machines for living," postmodernists speak of them gloomily as "human filing cabinets." Many of the trumpeted achievements of humanist social reform—such as criminal justice, welfare, and treatment of the mentally ill—have been shown to be ambiguous at best and counterproductive at worst. Modernist ideals built without God, such as "humanity," "truth," "freedom," and "justice," turn out to be highly precarious. They are vulnerable to being both dismissed as philosophically unfounded or attacked as the products of a particular culture or historical setting. Modernism, the postmodernists conclude, has been shattered by these problems. Along with it, the authority and status of intellectuals as the vanguard of modernity has also been shattered.

In contrast, postmodernism announces itself as a break with modernism just as modernism did earlier with tradition. Where modernism was a manifesto of human self-confidence and self-congratulation, postmodernism is a confession of modesty, if not despair. There is no truth, only truths. There are no principles, only preferences. There is no grand reason, only reasons. There is no privileged civilization (or culture, beliefs, norms, and styles), only a multiplicity of cultures, beliefs, periods, and styles. There is no universal justice, only interests and the competition of interest groups. There is no grand narrative of human progress, only countless stories of where people and their cultures are now. There is no simple reality or any grand objectivity of universal, detached knowledge, only a ceaseless representation of everything in terms of everything else.

In sum, postmodernism is a total repudiation of modernism and an extreme form of relativism. Paradoxically, it is almost an absolute relativism. If postmodernism is correct, we cannot even aspire after truth, objectivity, universality, and reality. As historian Gertrude Himmelfarb warned, "Postmodernism is the denial of the very idea of truth, reality, objectivity, reason or facts—all words which postmodernists now actually put in quotation marks! It's a totally permissive philosophy—anything goes—and it's extraordinary how far it has gone."[3]

Not Quite That Easy

Surprisingly, many Christians have welcomed postmodernism—because it clearly repudiates modernism. But this is naive, for Christians who welcome postmodernism have fallen prey to either or both of two fallacies.

One fallacy comes from *describing* postmodernism wrongly—as if modernity were only a set of ideas and not also a profound revolution in our social structures and institutions. If modernism and postmodernism are only sets of ideas, and if modernism has collapsed and postmodernism has prevailed, then modernity—the spirit and system of the world produced by modernism—is over along with all its challenges and dangers. Christians, and other religious believers and supporters of Western tradition, can breathe a sigh of relief.

If, however, modernity is not only a set of ideas but the product of such grand structural revolutions as capitalism, industrialized technology, and telecommunications, no relief is on the horizon. Modernism—as a set of ideas—may have collapsed but modernity—as a world system—is going strong.

Needless to say, the latter is true. Modernity cannot be explained by using the history of ideas alone. Modernism as a set of ideas may have collapsed and postmodernism as another set of ideas may have prevailed. But modernity, understood in its broader structural sense, is continuing without any interruption. Indeed, we are living at the high noon of modernity. Its challenges and dangers are stronger than ever. Christians who have prematurely declared victory over modernity are in for a cruel disillusionment.

The other fallacy comes from *assessing* postmodernism wrongly—even if it is mistaken as solely a set of ideas. It is true that modernism was openly hostile to religion and that postmodernism is much more sympathetic on the surface. But it is naive to ignore the price tag. Postmodern openness allows all religions and beliefs to present and practice their claims. But it demands the relinquishing of any claims to unique, absolute, and transcendent truth. For the Christian the cost is too high. Thus we can legitimately compare modernism and postmodernism as two sets of ideas and pronounce them as totally different. Or we can equally legitimately analyze postmodernism as the latest phase in the overall trajectory of modernity. Either way we can welcome the collapse of modernism and the exposure of its essential humanism. But we cannot pronounce that modernity is over. Neither can we overlook the fact that postmodernism is just as much a problem for the church as modernism.

Sometimes we will side with postmodernism against modernism. But we may just as often side with modernism against postmodernism. Like modernism, for example, Christians reject irrationalism. Like modernists, Christians defend truth, freedom, justice, and humanness as serious and universal. Modernism and postmodernism both have their insights, but both are equal dangers and equally inadequate half-truths. For Christians to join in the public flogging of the dying horse of modernism—thereby reinforcing the relativism and irrationalism of postmodernism and the acceleration of modernity itself—is fatuous and ironic.

HOPPING AND SHOPPING

This brief excursion into more rarefied issues is important because the greatest danger of postmodernism is in academia. Also there is great confusion as to what postmodernism and modernity are. But the rarefied discussion takes us away from the chief focus of this part of the book—the impact of modern culture on thinking at the popular level. Unquestionably the central impact of postmodernism on popular thinking is its philosophical reinforcement of the devouring, cannibalistic character of modern consumer culture.

Two metaphors are widely used in speaking of postmodernism—hopping and shopping. On the one hand, life in the postmodern world is television-channel hopping, with hand-held remote controls allowing us to graze at will in the flickering pastures of one greener channel after another. On the other hand, life in the postmodern world is shopping-mall or catalogue consumerism, allowing us to buy our way to a connoisseurship of surface and style. We pick out the bits and pieces of our consumer choice and assemble them into our own versions of who we are and how we live. Hence PoMo pioneer Barbara Krueger's celebration of consumer culture, "I Shop Therefore I Am" (1987). Hence the fact that we get fifty-two catalogues each year for every man, woman, and child in America. Hence the significance of advertising—it creates the world of pure image where all meanings are invented and images need only other images to give them meaning.

If postmodern style, such as Madonna's infamous video "Like a Prayer," is unsettling, it is meant to be. It uses and confuses. Often it plays. Sometimes it jokes. Commonly it parodies. Always it has irony. In the do-it-yourself spirit the past is blurred with the present, high culture with low culture, truth with lies, fiction with nonfiction, fact with fantasy, beliefs with games, ethical rules with social roles, museums with shopping malls, and comedy with violence. Life, after all, is a *TV Guide* of possibilities. Culture is a cross between a kaleidoscope, a grab bag, and a garage sale. There is no serious engagement or criticism. There is only ironic detachment. Playful self-consciousness is everything in the game of surfaces; serious interest in truth and depth is wasteful nostalgia.

The trademark gesture of postmodernism is not a handshake, a hug, or a punch. They are each too committed. It is a wink and a smirk. "I do everything," says Madonna, "with a wink."

Even at the height of the first Gilded Age, when wealthy Americans indulged in unprecedented cultural display, they were still admonished to be custodians of culture. At the dedication of the Metropolitan Museum in New York in 1880, Trustee Joseph C. Choate told his audience of "robber baron" millionaire industrialists and financiers:

> Think of it, ye millionaires of many markets—what glory may yet be yours, if you . . . [convert] the rude ores of commerce

into sculptured marble, and railroad shares and mining stocks—things which perish without the using—into the glorified canvas of the world's masters, that shall adorn these walls for centuries. The rage is to hunt the philosopher's stone, to convert all baser things into gold, which is but dross; but ours is the higher ambition to convert your useless gold into things of living beauty that shall be a joy to a whole people for a thousand years.[4]

Such highminded sentiments are unthinkable now in the Second Gilded Age. If truth, meaning, and reality have lost their status, the link between wealth and obligation has dissolved too. Whereas late nineteenth-century Americans were custodians of culture, we today—all of us, not simply millionaires—are cannibals of culture.

We are schooled in the lifestyle of creating and devouring things. Regardless of their truth, rightness, meaning, history, and value, anything and everything can be the victim of the all consuming image market. The Beatles's song "Revolution" becomes an advertisement for sneakers; dead writers like Friedrich Nietzsche and D. H. Lawrence offer quotations to sell beer; the Persian Gulf War sells Nintendo games; the second Russian Revolution sells vodka; the Statue of Liberty sells a myriad of products from deodorant to tobacco. Everything in postmodern America is up for sale. Everything is a matter of taste and style. Everything can be used for something else. The "do-your-own-thing" of the sixties has become the "create-your-own-reality" of the eighties and nineties—with multiple, Madonna-like reinventions always possible.

The implications of popular postmodernism for evangelical thinking need little elaboration. Popular PoMo is the ultimate modern reinforcement of the eight earlier pressures. For example, postmodernism reinforces the earlier impact of pietism because the postmodern church is no longer a community of truth or the bearer of a tradition privileged in American history; it is only one form of religious life among many forms of religious life. Or again, postmodernism reinforces the earlier impact of pluralism because the postmodern gospel is no longer a claim to truth but one story among many stories, one religious experience to be tasted among countless other tastings.

But perhaps postmodernism's main challenge to the church is to our central mission as Christians: following Christ and making him Lord in all of life. The church cannot become simply another customer center that offers designer religion and catalogue spirituality to the hoppers and shoppers of the modern world. Followers of Christ are custodians of the faith passed on down the running centuries. Never must we allow anyone outside or inside the church to become cannibals who devour the truth and meaning of this priceless heritage of faith. Letting the church be the church and the gospel be the gospel is integral to letting God be God.

14

TABLOID TRUTH

IN A LIVE INTERVIEW IN 1994 on ESPN's television show "Talk2," the host Jim Rome repeatedly insulted the New Orleans Saints's quarterback Jim Everett by calling him "Chris Evert." Obviously the reference was to the legendary women's tennis champion; the apparent motive was to insult the quarterback's toughness. Everett had a reputation, Rome explained later, for being a soft player who couldn't take a hit.

Rome had evidently used the nickname many times before, both on radio and television, but never to Everett's face. When Rome did it again, Everett warned him not to. But when Rome persisted Everett overturned the table between them and sent Rome sprawling on the floor. He was standing over him when a producer intervened and the camera cut away.

"I don't regret what I did," Jim Everett said in self-defense. "I was put in a position that I thought was going to be a journalistic-type interview and, instead, I was put into what I felt was a taunting attack."[1] But Jim Rome was equally unapologetic in defense of his show. "It was not malicious. It was all in good fun, verbal jousting. . . 'Talk2' is a 'mix of entertainment and journalism.' "[2]

Clearly one man's "taunting attack" was another man's "good fun" and everyone's good entertainment. In this case the host's tactics backfired because the guest broke the talk-show rules and did what came naturally to him on the football field. The host, however, was just acting in character—Rome's "ripping athletes" on his show helped build up his cult following in the Los Angeles area.

But Rome's rationale about "entertainment and journalism" is a wider recurring theme on radio and television today. It also contributes to a style of discourse that could be called "tabloid truth" or "talk-show truth," which in turn is pressuring the Christian mind in America today. For one key to the "idiot culture," as Carl Bernstein and others have described it, is "the emergence of a talk-show nation in which public discourse is reduced to ranting and raving and posturing."[3]

Supermarket scandal sheets have been around for a long time. They are tirelessly ingenious in pressing the boundaries of the bizarre, grotesque, and outrageous. But until recently a reassuring fire wall was erected between these back-alley freak shows and respectable Main Street journalism. But with the arrival of "tabloid television" and the "gawk shows," and with the rising incidence of such scandal-reporting in mainstream journalism, including the networks, the fire wall has grown dangerously thin.

Needless to say, "tabloid truth" is only one of many cancers eating at public discourse. But most of the other practical causes—such as direct mail and sound bites—have been given far more attention. Equally, the roots of tabloid journalism are not solely American. As an Englishman I am embarrassed to admit that the traditions of the London press have to a considerable extent been imported into the United States by British journalists and Australian newspaper owners.

TRUTH AS POWER PLAY

But tabloid truth is emerging in a distinctively American form to become a prime shaper of American thinking and discourse. Its two most prominent ingredients are selling and sensationalism. A third ingredient is a rampant form of voyeurism and envy that is the primary appeal of tabloid style. As journalist Henry Fairlie noted,

It is well understood that to take away someone's good name is second only to murder as an offense against them; it is itself a way of destroying them. The gossip column is the symbol of an envious age, and so is the contemporary form of interview, which seems designed to ensure in the same manner as the gossip column, that virtue and talent and achievement will be reduced to the level at which we can feel we are their equal. They are "just like us," even a little lower than us.[4]

But behind those three factors is another more serious ingredient—the crisis of truth. Public figures are an obvious casualty of tabloid truth—once fingered and besmirched, their reputation is sometimes beyond repair. But when every story is bought and sold, sometimes for extraordinary sums of money, truth itself is the principal victim. In the Michael Jackson alleged child-molesting scandal, for example, even his parents agreed to be interviewed—for a payment of $100,000.

Yet truth-for-a-price is only one part of the assault on truth. Another is the concept of truth-as-power-play. With the crisis of the notion of objective truth at the philosophical level, claims to truth have collapsed into expressions of the will to power. The crisis of truth can assume tribal forms, such as multicultural conflicts on campus where truth-as-power-play can lead to real violence and severe discrimination.

But the crisis can also take tabloid form, as on radio and television, where there is an open license for truth-as-power-play but where it typically remains entertainment—at least for the audience. The witty put-downs, taunts, and near-assassinations of character flirt dangerously with the boundaries of taste and ethics. But they can always be excused by the ever-elastic fallback category of "entertainment." (Jim Rome's "verbal jousting" as "good fun" in the service of "entertainment and journalism.")

In the meantime, of course, truth-as-power-play is a potent weapon in the service of those with a cause to promote or a program to sell. We might therefore say of Rush Limbaugh and Howard Stern, the Tweedledum and Tweedledee of the current talk-show spectrum, that because they are so brilliantly the epitome of today's media, if they did not exist, they would have to be invented.

One reason for the power of tabloid and talk-show truth is that it coincides with the emergence of "virtual communities," almost-but-not-really-communities coalescing around the new technologies of communication. The near-universal appeal of traditional network television, for example, has splintered under the impact of the new technologies. People now want their own sources of information and their own styles of communication— usually from like-minded people, stated in their own in-house language, uncensored and unchallenged. Thus rock musician Ice-T has described rap music as "the black CNN" because it keeps people aware of life on the streets. In the same tenor it is not hard to feel the sense of "community" surrounding homosexual rights, the religious Right, or the followers of "Rush" and "Howard."

The overall result of tabloid and talk-show truth is one more nail in the coffin of serious speech in search of truth. Vaporized by endless critical theories about its nature, twisted by ideologies, replaced by psychological categories, obscured by suffocating clouds of euphemism and jargon, outpaced by rumor and hype, overlooked for the dazzling appeal of style and image— and now subject to selling, jousting, and entertainment in the press and media—truth in America is anything but marching on. As historian William Lee Miller has observed, Jefferson's belief that truth is great and will prevail is today "more a prayer than an axiom."[5]

Some principled calls for more responsible public language have been heard. Some are on behalf of individuals. Actor Richard Gere and supermodel Cindy Crawford, for example, placed a $30,000 full-page advertisement in *The Times* of London in May 1994. They were denying rumors that their marriage was on the rocks. "Thoughts and words are very powerful so please be responsible, thoughtful, and kind," they pleaded.

Other calls are more general. It has become clear, for example, that trading insults and taunting names ("fighting words") is a serious factor in inner-city teen violence. Stopping abusive language is therefore a key part of stopping abuse. For the most part, however, the practical limits are not ethical but commercial. Radio talk-show host Howard Stern, for instance, has been attacked as sexist, racist, and indecent. But even when his on-air outrages have met with million-dollar fines, his program has been too lucrative to be cut. When the bottom line is what matters, there is unquestionably good business in bad taste.

THE GOSPEL AND THE GAWK SHOWS

Has tabloid and talk-show truth influenced Christian thinking and discourse? Direct impact would be difficult to pin down, but points of convergence are easy to see. First, many Christians have become consumers of the popular talk shows with the same entertainment-minded unconcern for truth as many other consumers. This problem surfaces repeatedly among devoted followers of such conservative media personalities as Rush Limbaugh and Oliver North. It is one thing to glory in the culture warring— "We love them for the enemies they have made." It is another to miss the fact that truth and justice are frequent casualties of such barnstorming entertainment.

One of the privileges of being an author is the flow of letters and phone calls one receives from around the country and around the world. For example, at the time of President Clinton's victory in the presidential elections in 1992, many wrote and called to express their alarm. Did the Democratic victory presage the end times, as one person wrote? Had the moment arrived, as another put it, for a "second Mayflower"—this time sailing *from* America, not to it?

But one characteristic was striking in the alarm and gloom in the letters and calls. The Bible supplied the metaphors for the alarm—the "end times" and so on. But the real authority they looked to was Rush Limbaugh. It was always, "Rush Limbaugh said," "Did you hear what Rush Limbaugh said," or simply, "I believe Rush Limbaugh." Many of Limbaugh's audience speak of "discovering" him almost as a conversion experience and their enthusiasm to share "the faith" almost as a form of witnessing.

Modern media personalities are not for the ages—Andy Warhol's "fifteen minutes in the sun" is operative. But where is Christian discernment? Never mind that Rush Limbaugh voted for the first time in a presidential election only in 1988, when he was forty-seven years old. This was a full eight years after Reagan's election and twenty-four after the launch of the conservative revolution. Never mind that his entertaining style often overpowers his seriousness. Never mind the mounting evidence of a less than rigorous dedication to facts and verification.[6]

In the age of talk-show punditry, it is fatuous that "Thus sayeth Rush" (or anyone else) is as inerrant and canonical as Scripture. As Garrison Keillor, another much-loved media personality, said gently, "It must be fun to say what Rush Limbaugh says, but imagine having to believe it and base your life on it."[7]

Second, Christian discourse is beginning to take on some of the characteristics of tabloid and talk-show truth. For a start, we have our own frenzied circulation of myths and "psychofacts"—beliefs that become true because we feel they are true, even if they are not; or beliefs that are not supported by hard evidence but are taken as real because their constant repetition changes the way we view life. A current example is the carefully contrived, skillfully engineered myth that Christians are "a small persecuted minority victimized by 'liberal elites.' "

Further, we have our own Christian forms of truth-as-powerplay. Whereas liberals, who are often a minority, tend to resort to the courts in the absence of persuasion, Christian conservatives, who are often a majority, tend to resort to crusades. Proclamations, protests, pronouncements, picketing—the purpose and style of communication is anything but persuasion. Thus good lawsuits on the one side and good "wars" on the other have substituted a good cause.

In the Bible military metaphors are mostly used in connection with supernatural warfare. For example, the Apostle Paul: "The weapons we fight with are not the weapons of the world.

On the contrary, they have divine power to demolish strong-holds."[8] Legal metaphors, by contrast, more commonly refer to people—hearts and minds are to be won rather than an enemy to be annihilated. For example, the Apostle Peter: "Always be pre-pared to give an answer [apologia] to everyone who asks you to give the reason for the hope that you have. But do this with gentleness and respect."[9] But many Christians today have oblit-erated that distinction. The military has overpowered the legal. Persuasion based on truth is irrelevant; no-hostages-taken, power-play communication is now the name of the game.

Similarly, the early church recognized that it was legitimate to hate evil. God does and so must we—but only so long as we love God and love the evil-doing neighbor even more than we hate the evil. Yet listen to the rhetoric of many talk shows on Christian radio today. Enemy-bashing is common. Outright evil, anti-Chris-tian enemy-hating is far from rare. The triumph of tabloid and talk-show truth is sadly evident in the church of Christ.

Years after the Spanish civil war, George Orwell used to tell the tale of his refusal to kill a fascist soldier. Crawling close to the enemy trenches, he caught a fascist in his rifle sights who was holding up his trousers as he ran. Orwell could not pull the trig-ger. "I had come here to shoot at 'Fascists'; but a man who is holding up his trousers isn't a 'Fascist', he is visibly a fellow crea-ture."[10] Would that the world could witness similar humanity and compassion today from those who worship the Creator of humanity and serve the Author of compassion.

RENT-A-MOB FOR JESUS

Two special features of contemporary Christian discourse are notable. One is the fact that Christian television is frequently much more violent in its rhetoric than its secular counterpart. Able to presume on an audience that is unified and partisan, Christian television has none of the economic constraints that silence secular television in a pluralistic society. And it often appears to have no theological restraint either. In more than twenty-five years of visiting the United States and more than ten living here, I have received several threatening death pronouncements—purportedly relayed from "on high." But the most egregious and public examples of violent rhetoric are from the Faith teachers. They pronounce divine judgment on those who dare question their so-called prophetic ministry.

One Faith teacher ominously warned the critics of his message, "There will be those who don't accept it and will fall dead in the pulpit."[11] Another declared on national television that he wished he could blow off the heads of his "stinking" enemies with a "Holy Ghost machine gun."[12] The same pastor said a year later at a mammoth rally, "The Holy Ghost is upon me. . . . The day is coming when those that attack us will drop dead. You say, 'What did you say?' I speak this under the anointing of the Spirit. Can I tell you something? Don't touch God's servants; it's deadly. . . . Woe to you that touch God's servants. You're going to pay."[13]

A second feature of contemporary Christian discourse is its relationship to heresy hunting. The pressures of modern media have created a real catch-22 when it comes to maintaining orthodoxy. On the one hand, the need for theological vigilance is greater than ever. We evangelicals have no binding creed or covenant, we discount truth and theology, and our most prominent leaders and institutions are largely silent about heresy. So our present capacity for speculation, heresy, and blasphemy appears to grow boundless. We are therefore indebted to such people as R. C. Sproul, Michael Horton, and Hank Hanegraaff, and all whose calling is to expose and combat error.

On the other hand, we are now witnessing a malignant mutation of the tabloid-truth trend in the emergence of a technopopulist form of evangelical witchhunting. Populism and self-appointed heresy hunting have long gone hand in hand, but mostly at the fringes of evangelicalism. The new technologies, however, are changing this because they coincide with the absence of strong, responsible evangelical leadership and the emergence of technologically linked "virtual communities" of frustration, fear, and rage.

With the use of e-mail, fax machines, and desktop publishing as well as radio and television, what were once the "rent-a-mob" propaganda tactics of the left-wing can now be marshaled against any Christian leader, speaker, or writer with whom one disagrees. In the process a genuine Christian concern for truth, orthodoxy, fidelity, and accountability has degenerated into vile campaigns of rumor, slander, disinformation, and vilification. Where talk-show truth at the more benign level represents a shift from exposition to entertainment, the malignant version is a shift from exposition to exposé that is typical of the tabloid press at its worst and utterly unworthy of a community that bears the name of Christ.

When all is said and done, tabloid and talk-show truth is no truth at all. Rather it is a form of power games set in an entertaining commercial mode. Nothing could be farther from the grace and truth that Jesus spoke and lived. "Doing God's work in God's way" poses special challenges in the days of the "shock jocks," the "gawk shows," and the exponents of hard-core exposés.

15

~⁓⁓⁓~

GENERATION HEX

When Nelson Mandela visited the United States in 1990 after his decades of political imprisonment, entrepreneurs manufactured a line of T-shirts bearing Mandela's likeness with slogans of black unity. One caused widespread comment. It read, "IT'S A BLACK THING. YOU WOULDN'T UNDERSTAND." Some of the reactions were strongly critical. Martin Luther King would have repudiated such a message, critics said. "It's a human thing," he would have trumpeted: "You'd better understand."

Others pointed out the naturalness of the new sense of tribalism. Only those within a group can know what it is like to be a member of the group, they say, so those outside have no right to comment or criticize. To do so is to be insensitive and show disrespect. Seen this way, the sad mixture of resignation and defiance was understandable but the tribalism is not unique to African-Americans. In today's setting, with the vogue for multiculturalism, many other words could be inserted instead of "black"—"It's a Jewish/feminist/gay/lesbian/fundamentalist/physically challenged thing. You wouldn't understand."

But recent decades have witnessed the rise of a new kind of tribalism—generational tribalism, as members of a similar age are given—or give themselves—cute, all-inclusive names designed to be the logo of their times. Having barely survived a deluge of discussion about the baby boomers—those born between 1946 and 1964—we now witness a frenzied search to

name the succeeding generation of postboomer-premillenials
born during the sixties and seventies. Yet despite all the hot air emitted and the ink spilled by
countless trendsetters and marketing executives, no name has
yet stuck. But the list of hopefuls is long. "Baby busters" (as in
"from boom to bust") was never attractive. But nothing else has
captured the majority imagination either. "The New Lost Generation" (*Time* Magazine), "Twentysomethings," "Generation X"
(from Douglas Coupland's novel of the same title), "13ers" (from
the thirteenth generation to come of age since Benjamin
Franklin), the "Angry Generation" (because of divorce, AIDS,
crime, and joblessness), or more simply latchkeys, technobabies,
cyborgs, posties, mall rats, nowheres, burnouts—the list is endless
and the task appears hopeless.

The bandwagon vogue for age-egocentrism and generational
apartheid appears to have run into hopeless difficulties. When
Kurt Cobain, lead singer and songwriter of the Seattle grunge rock
band Nirvana, committed suicide in 1994, many labeled him as
the "voice of his generation." But he himself had been utterly disdainful of such a role. As many of his fans insisted, they were different from their predecessors precisely because they had no voice.
All they believed in was that there was nothing to believe in. To
pretend otherwise was to collude with the marketing executives
and insult the individuality of their peers. Perhaps, as one young
person put it, we are simply "Generation Hex," the generation
cursed by all the bewitching nonsense about generations.

Generational tribalism is a sixth important pressure influ-
encing Christian thinking—one that Christians must understand
rather than simply reflect uncritically, if they are not to fall into
the lazy distortions that characterize such a way of seeing things.

GENERATIONAL FASHION DESIGNERS

Definition by generation is a distinctive phenomenon of the
twentieth century, which many historians have traced to the
1920s. There were, of course, earlier prefigurings of the devel-

opment. Jefferson, for example, wrote of the need for a new American revolution every twenty years and Tocqueville had observed how each generation in a democracy was a new people. But four things emerged in the 1920s to give us our present sense of generational tribalism.

First was an awareness of greatly accelerated change and a preoccupation with a sense of "progress." Caused by a combination of factors—World War I, technological advances, and dramatic cultural changes—a yawning chasm appeared to open between one generation and the next. Those born prior to the chasm appeared to inhabit a world of innocence, those after it a world of lost innocence.

Second was an awareness of "nostalgia" as the flipside of progress. Originating in the Greek word for "homesickness," nostalgia previously was almost exclusively a medical term. Suddenly it became popular and signified a sense of homesickness for a lost age and a lost innocence. Naturally, this lost innocence was a matter of perception as much as reality—the 1920s saw themselves as radical, bitter, and cynical, but that did not prevent the 1930s from using an air-brushed, rose-tinted version of the 1920s for images of nostalgia in the later decade.

Third was a new fascination with decades, later called "decadology." The ten-year period became the standard unit by which to identify shifting styles, fashions, and moods. Hence the "roaring twenties" (or "lost generation"), the "fabulous forties" (or "war generation"), the "golden fifties" (or the "silent generation"), the "seismic sixties" (or the "Vietnam generation"), and so on.

Fourth was a growing sense of "generation wars." Each generation was thought to be constituted by the solidarity of its shared events and experiences. Among the defining memories of such "tribes" are its political acts and assassinations, its heroes of sport and music, and a lesser melange of its childhood television shows and historic rock concerts. Each generation has therefore tended to view the entire century from the perspective of its own generation, setting itself off against those just ahead and all following.

The results of this new generational awareness were unsurprising—a dramatic shortening of historical attention, the creation of a new solidarity of identity and style, a heightening of the tensions between generations, and an acceleration of the turnover between generations, decades, and styles. Thus generational identities and styles became subject to the fashions and frustrations of the market just as much as Detroit's new models in cars.

For all its dangers, however, we must not dismiss this generational tribalism too fast. For a start, it is partly inevitable. As the accelerating changes and choices of modernity seem to speed up history, such older categories as income and class appear too static and outworn. Such time-defined units of identification as generations became natural. Definition by birth-year seems fitting to people whose traditional ties of family, church, and neighborhood no longer hold.

More importantly, the notion of generation is profoundly biblical and takes its place alongside other key terms, such as "time," "age," "hour," and "moment." In each case, chronological time matters little. What counts is not the passage of time, but its purpose under providence. What makes a difference is not the succession of moments but the significance of the moment. Thus in Luke chapter seven, for example, Jesus repeatedly refers to "this generation." A far cry from our modern age-tribes, "generation" as Jesus uses it addresses the solidarity and responsibility of all those alive on the earth at a particular time.

Modern generational awareness is trivial when compared with the biblical understanding. Christians should therefore think twice before picking up the categories, either as a serious effort in identification or as a bid to be relevant, up-to-date, or "seeker friendly." For one thing, generational identifications are too often distorting. Vague and simplistic at their best, they can easily pander to those too lazy to think for themselves and create a reductionist form of labeling.

It is as if we find that people without a nametag are threatening to us, so we rush to put on any old nametag to provide an instant ID card, making possible our continuing relationship.

That method works, of course, so long as both the speaker and the listener accept the same shorthand and so long as the expiration date on the label has not run out. But when the old label becomes obsolete, people are stuck with clichés that do not communicate and with categories that are too sweeping to address the real needs of the real individuals in front of their noses. This has happened recently with Christians mouthing generalizations about "boomers" just as boomers became more and more restless about the generalizations foisted upon them.

For another thing, generational identifications often mask a great deal of self-interest. We all see the world from our own perspective, whether as individuals or as generations. Nothing, then, is more natural than to see all history as leading up to our own insight—or interest. It is no accident that generational tribalism is fostered supremely by marketing executives (and in the church-growth movement by missionary marketers). The rush to define is a rush to package and sell.

As change accelerates, the ironies mount. On the one hand, there is a splintering effect. The generational tag lines become more regional and short-lived, covering fewer and fewer people. On the other hand, resistance also mounts. The advertisers' motives become so transparent and the periodic scramble to label becomes so fatuous that more and more people resist labels altogether. Not unnaturally, they prefer just to be themselves.

A common error about the Christian mind is the notion that it is only about belief and doctrine. As we shall see, it is about far, far more. The Christian mind bears on everything that Christ's truth bears upon—which is quite simply everything, including the very distinctive and vital biblical sense of time.

There are important convergences between the Christian and the contemporary views of time. But there are also major differences. Not to recognize their differences is to fall for another of the bewitching pressures of our culture. Christians can learn much from the restiveness of the "twentysomething" young person frustrated at being pinned down and exploited as Generation Hex.

16

REAL, REEL, OR VIRTUALLY REAL?

IN DECEMBER 1993 A YOUNG Virginia college student slumped onto the wheel of his car as he drove down Highway 17. He swerved into a truck and was killed instantly. What was to blame? Alcohol? Drugs? Pressure of work? A medical problem? None of the above. He had simply gone sleepless for almost a week in his passion to enter the world of "AmberMUSH," a multiuser computer network dedicated to role-playing games.

In real life the young Virginian was awkward, shy, and had unspectacular high-school grades. But on-line he was as different as anyone could possibly be—a desirable but treacherous, manipulative, and street-savvy woman called Sabbath. Always a target for teasing and bullying when growing up, he developed into a consummate "game boy" for whom being on-line was a lifeline to existence itself. Then, as family and friends said later, the fantasy and role-playing world became so completely real that he all but quit real life and moved into cyberspace. Finally, the terminal became terminal.

PERSON-TO-PERSON IS NOT FACE-TO-FACE

We cannot make grand generalizations from a personal tragedy like this one. But a recurring theme emerged from the many responses to news of his death. Part of the appeal of cybercommunication is that it is person-to-person but not face-to-face.

125

Although its collective illusion-making requires high role-playing skills and highly developed rules of on-line conduct, it gives license for free expression of the imagination and emotion while always preserving privacy.

The AmberMUSH program manager explained its appeal: Such systems give users "a chance to step outside the usual boundaries of social constraint. . . . Age, gender, economic background, sexual preference, ethnic background and political belief are completely irrelevant. . . . You can confide in sympathetic strangers with the confidence of complete anonymity. You can question things you've been taught without being treated as some kind of flake. You can hear views from types of people that you'd otherwise never meet, people from outside your geographical location, involved in jobs or hobbies that you've never heard of."[1]

Concerns about cyberspace and the new information superhighway are surrounded by a swirl of hype and anxiety, starry-eyed utopian claims, and dark Luddite premonitions. But one thing is undeniable: the latest developments in communication technology have challenging implications for our experience and understanding of truth and human personality. As such they represent another powerful modern pressure bearing down on the Christian mind.

If the past is any guide, the outcome of the computer revolution will probably lie somewhere between the optimists and the pessimists. At the present moment the cyberboosters are out in force, from Vice President Gore downward. Such new communication technologies as video telephones, they tell us, will actually help "repair the family." The new styles of life that result, such as telecommuting, will "restore the lost sense of community." The new communication tools, they announce to us with deadpan earnestness, will make human life more human.

It is difficult, however, to be impressed. The television revolution was announced with the same fanfare. Commercial television, it was predicted in the forties, would "strengthen family ties" and make "cities unnecessary." It would allow high culture and the arts to permeate the whole of society. It would provide a democratic people with a "cultural uplift" beyond the reach of any in the past below the elite. Above all, as it has been said of new technologies for over two hundred years, it would make possible the magic dream of "the leisure society."

Interactive TV, movies on demand, video games, databases, educational programming, home shopping, telebanking, virtual reality of all kinds—cybergurus gush with all the wonders of new information services for ordinary people. But it is hard to escape some fundamental suspicions—that we will have even less leisure than before, that many people will have an even higher anxiety because of the higher complexity, and that the popular level of applications will witness more cultural trash than excellence.

In sum, what the hardware makes possible, the software will make real. And the signs are that commercially viable software will—to put it charitably—rise no higher in artistic and intellectual excellence than the mediocrity of television during the past fifty years. The fruitful union between high technology and the trashiness of the "idiot culture" is not likely to end in divorce soon.

THE ESPERANTO OF OUR TIME

Perhaps the sharpest challenges to the Christian mind come from the tools and styles of "virtual reality." At first restricted largely to entertainment arcades, virtual-reality technologies are predicted that will constitute a new form of human experience— "a lift-off into electronic space," as its proponents modestly claim.

Virtual reality (or VR) technology is still at a rudimentary stage, but those enamored by it become breathless at its godlike capacities—the verisimilitude of the simulation, the all-embracing immersion of the environment, and the near-omniscience of the "hypertext" potential for interpreting any text. If the medieval tradition was human thinking reduced to logical reasoning, modern communication is human knowledge and experience reduced to information processing. The calculus of digital information is the esperanto of our time—or the nearest we can get to it. We may not all speak the same language, but a universal calculus can bring all human languages into a single, shared database.

As one critic puts it, human knowledge now approaches the "omniscient intuitive cognition of the deity."[2] No temporal unfolding, no linear steps, no delays—the latest technologies bring us to the threshold of the all-at-onceness of instant, total information and godlike simulation.

Is the new cybertechnology simply a tool or is it a menace to our humanness? Is our modern love affair with computers merely a matter of intellectual fascination? Or is it, as some have said, erotic—a deep spiritual and sensuous search for a home for our minds and hearts? Does cyberspace represent such an enhancement of the mind at the expense of the body—to the point where the body is optional—that it amounts to a new gnosticism? Does it matter that machine-mediated "telepresence" and the "on-line community" lack the immediacy and responsibility of face-to-face linear sharing?

Only time will answer these questions, but my main concern for the impact of cyberspace on Christian thinking concerns the issues of truth and reality. Technically, "virtual reality" signifies an event or experience that is real in effect but not in fact. Virtual reality, in other words, is a humanly constructed technological world that combines two things: a high degree of realism in simulation and a high degree of interaction that amounts to total immersion. Thus the term "virtual reality" was chosen by its inventors—and avoided by its critics—because of its powerful metaphysical promise. Virtual reality is the Holy Grail of the creative power of technology.

"Is it real or reel?" That question from a generation ago was designed to help children distinguish facts from fantasy on television and thus to make them "literate" in watching television. The power of virtual reality suspends such questions altogether and takes us to another world. Virtual reality is still at a crude level today, but the promise of its progress beckons us to a higher level—a level closer to what Richard Wagner had in mind with his concept of the "total work of art" at the Bayreuth Festival.

When Wagner completed his last opera *Parsifal*, he no longer saw it simply as opera, or even music, theatre, and art—and certainly not as "entertainment." He was rivaling a high Catholic mass. He was creating an artificial reality that could become a total experience, which in turn would transform ordinary reality and experience. The final purpose was nothing less than religious.

Today's virtual reality is a far cry from Wagner's high art—thank God, for Hitler's Nuremberg rallies mimicked Wagner as astutely as anyone. Doubtless virtual reality in the future will achieve its own Bayreuth simulations. Doubtless the road will also be littered with simulations that are far trashier, more trivial, and less pretentious. But the overall tendency is likely to undermine the status of reality and truth further still. Personal fantasy, stories, novels, and films already move us from one dimension of reality to another—and properly so. But the shift represented by virtual reality is a quantum leap into artificiality and relativism, a major defiance of the finiteness and fallenness of reality as seen within the Christian view of the world.

KEEPING VIRTUAL REALITY VIRTUAL

How can we keep virtual reality virtual? Is it possible that tomorrow's technologies will allow us to slip the leash of mundane reality enough to create the illusion of a reality beyond rootedness? Cybergnosticism would be the outcome of such flights of fancy, for the ultimate VR experience of the future will aim to be spiritually sublime. Doubtless, too, we can expect the crasser but highly imaginative sections of Christian commerce to produce not only "The VR Battle of Armageddon" but "Virtual Conversions," "Virtual Quiet Times," "Virtual Mystical Experiences," and on-line "Virtual Recovery Groups."

The higher end of the development of virtual reality raises profound philosophical and religious questions. As Michael Heim warns, "An unrestrained proliferation of worlds cries out for sanity, for connection with reality, for metaphysical grounding."[3] But the lower end will have the greater impact. The biblical view of reality is gloriously realistic—human life from ashes to ashes and dust to dust lived out in the form of blood, sweat, and tears.

Before long we can expect the cyberbodies of tomorrow's virtual reality to suffer the expected disorders that are the advances on today's jet lag and simulator sickness. Christian reality will then be the last best reality check on virtual-reality systems. But this is only if Christians are still shaped by the decisively different truth and reality in which we believe. The magic kingdom of "virtual Christianity" may have a market, but it has no future.

THE FIRE ALARM AND THE ARSONIST

As I stressed at the beginning of Part Two, this brief survey of eight cultural pressures is not comprehensive. Many other pressures could be cited—for example, the influence of psychology at the popular level (Philip Rieff's "triumph of the therapeutic"). Nor should anyone draw false conclusions from these warnings.

One false conclusion is that I must be opposed to any or all of these things—television, advertising, style, talk shows, generation talk, virtual reality, postmodernism, psychology, and so on. As Marshall McLuhan used to say, "I feel a bit like the man who turns in a fire alarm only to be charged with arson."[4] McLuhan's descriptions of the effects of technology, in other words, inclined people—wrongly—to regard him as the enemy of the things he described. So also here. I am opposed only to the negative effects of these things. Modernity, however, is always double-edged and I could as easily write about its benefits rather than its costs.

A second false conclusion is that any critic of these trends, myself included, can easily resist the trends themselves. It is never that easy. Even Norman Mailer, lamenting the fate of the serious novel, admitted recently that "very few" of his nine children "are more conversant with my work than they are with the people on television."[5] He confessed he had been reduced to bribing his youngest son to read ten novels by promising him two hours of television a day if he did—a venture that was not wholly successful.

A third false conclusion is that these pressures are abstract and inconsequential—too intellectual and remote to make much difference. Far from it. We have already examined the scandal and the sin—evangelical ineffectiveness in public life, for example. Let me add here a further consequence: the growing degradation of Christian thinking into speculation, heresy, blasphemy, and just plain weirdness.

Many evangelicals were rightly shocked and incensed at the liberal Protestant "Re-Imagining," the "Global Theological Conference by Women" held in Minneapolis in 1993. Presentations deriding orthodoxy and denying the atonement of Jesus Christ, a standing ovation for lesbians, a service of milk and honey to the goddess Sophia—what is left of "mainline Protestantism" was flaunting some of the vilest heresies that have ever reared their heads in the church of Christ in two thousand years.

Yet what many evangelicals fail to recognize and protest is the similar movement growing in conservative circles. Listen carefully to the Faith teachers. The theology, politics, and cultural style are different, but the heresy, blasphemy, and weirdness are the same. Paganism is growing up in our churches. Speculative gnosticism is resurgent in our own circles. A horror of great darkness is welling up in our own house. Yet judging by the way heresy is published and marketed by respected evangelical houses and watched and read by millions of good evangelical viewers and readers, we evangelicals love to have it so. And this is only the beginning of the degradation of evangelical thinking that is coming unless we experience reformation.

Our task, as followers of Christ, is not easy but it is clear: The challenge, in St. Paul's words, is to "not conform any longer to the pattern of this world, but be transformed by the renewing of your mind."[6] Thus the currents are swift and the pressures strong, but a focus on the negative is far from negative. It is the first step to the most glorious positive of all, having the mind of Christ.

PART THREE

LET MY PEOPLE THINK

ONE OF THE MOST CELEBRATED PERSONALITIES of the Middle East is Nasreddin Hodja, the endearing holy-man-cum-scholar of Turkish folklore. His famed wisdom is often threatened by his equally famed stupidity. One day, so a particular story goes, the Hodja dropped his ring inside his house. Not finding it there, he went outside and began to look around the doorway. His neighbor passed and asked him what he was looking for.

"I have lost my ring," said the Hodja.

"Where did you lose it?" asked the neighbor.

"In my bedroom," said the Hodja.

"Then why are you looking for it out here?"

"There's more light out here," the Hodja said.

Perhaps the Hodja in his frankly acknowledged folly is wiser than most of us in the concealed stupidity of our pretended wisdom. It is surely the easiest thing to look for what we lost where we lost it—except that humans characteristically either forget what we lost or look for it anywhere except where it can be found.

This is certainly true of the Christian mind, or, more simply, just of wisdom. Exactly what it is, where we lost it, and how we can find it again are urgent but basic questions.

I say that because we could easily examine "the ghost mind" of evangelicalism and its vulnerability to "the idiot culture" and then be sidetracked by the grand cultural questions raised, especially the political.

132

Plainly, all we have looked at represents a momentous challenge for the American republic. From the Greeks onward it has long been recognized that the inherent vice of democracy is corruption from within, so that democracy slumps into anarchy. Such a process of leveling (or "dumbing-down") as we are seeing is therefore immensely significant. Neil Postman, for instance, argues soberly that "Watching political commercials is hazardous to the intellectual health of the community."[1] Indeed, he warns, "the television commercial has mounted the most serious assault on capitalist ideology since the publication of *Das Kapital*."[2]

I have no quarrel with Postman's argument, nor with the logic of his warning that we are producing a culture similar to the "bread and circuses" (or mass consumption and mass spectacle) of Juvenal's Rome.

But at that point the Christian citizen—which includes Postman, Ellul, and many of the most astute observers we have followed—parts company with most other citizens. For the deepest answers begin neither with politics and programs nor with the paraphernalia of the big, the strategic, and the abstract. Although our answers may include these things at a later stage, they begin with the nature of wisdom, the Christian mind, and of thinking Christianly.

We therefore turn in Part Three to sketching the rudiments of the needed reformation in evangelical thinking. The word "sketched" should be underscored. What is outlined briefly here deserves a book by itself. But an introductory sketch is important to spell out what is meant by "thinking Christianly" and—equally important—what is not meant by it.

BACK TO OUR RIGHT MINDS

The first step in reformation is repentance. We evangelicals need to confess individually and collectively that we have betrayed the Great Commandment to love God with our minds. We need to confess that we have given ourselves up to countless forms of unutterable folly. God has given us minds, but many of us have left them underdeveloped or undeveloped. God has given us education, beyond that of most people in human history, but we have used it for other ends. God has given us great exemplars of thinking in Christian history, but we have ignored them or admired them for other virtues. God has given us opportunities, but we have failed to grasp them because we have refused to think them through before him.

As we think of not only our individual lives but our evangelical heritage, community as a whole, reputation in the wider world, and prospects—and as we survey the old and new influences that have shaped us, whether the eight earlier influences or the eight modern pressures—we must ask some key questions. Are we as truly biblical as we think? Have we not been more shaped by the world than we realize? Would we see it more clearly if brothers and sisters of other traditions, such as Catholics, pointed it out to us? Or former evangelicals who have dropped out from the faith altogether? Is there any question that we evangelicals have often stressed every other possible Christian theme except those of truth and thinking? Can we deny that American evangelicals have a long and unbroken history of pervasive and systematic anti-intellectualism? In short, who can disagree with the sorry fact that our evangelical anti-intellectualism confronts us today as a monumental scandal and a sin?

It is not for me to say how repentance should be expressed. Doubtless sometimes it will have to be by individuals, sometimes by local pastors and churches, sometimes by Christian organizations and ministries, sometimes by Christian magazines, and sometimes by Christian colleges. And surely in a wise and responsible way it will need to be confessed by the official, national organs and institutions of evangelicalism itself.

But repentance at this point has to be as serious and far-reaching as repentance at any other point. Like Nebuchadnezzar who had to be reduced to eating grass, or the prodigal son who only saw his situation in the mirror that was the pigsty, we may have to be jolted by the shame of our present sorry state into returning to our right minds. For it is certain that the community of faith in America that identifies itself as evangelical has been out of its mind for two hundred years.

MINDS IN LOVE

The second step in reformation is to define what we actually mean by "a Christian mind" or by "thinking Christianly." Obviously, for example, the term "thinking Christianly" has two parts that require serious attention. Thus we must first ask what we mean by "thinking." For as Dorothy L. Sayers laments in her celebrated essay, "The Lost Tools of Learning," "Is not the great defect of our education today . . . that although we often succeed in teaching our pupils 'subjects,' we fail lamentably on the whole in teaching them how to think: they learn everything, except the art of learning."[3] In my experience no single point of cultural differences between America and England is greater than this one: in English schooling we were given the tools of learning and were taught to think.

My focus here, however, is not on "thinking" but "thinking Christianly." Because of the deep confusion over what is meant, some negative statements must precede the positive. First, thinking Christianly is not thinking by Christians. As a moment's thought will show, it is perfectly possible to be a Christian and yet to think in a sub-Christian or even an anti-Christian way. Jesus said bluntly to his disciple Peter, "Away with you, Satan. You think as men think, not as God thinks."[4]

Second, thinking Christianly is not simply thinking about Christian topics. Such topics as prayer, Bible study, and the spiritual disciplines all fall within the bounds of recognizable Christian themes. Thus they are surely candidates to be part of the Christian mind. But the trouble with that approach is that it leaves out the greater part of life. The nineteenth-century maxim applies not only to theology but to life as a whole: "If Jesus Christ is not Lord of all, he is not Lord at all."

Third, thinking Christianly should not be confused with adopting a "Christian line" on every issue. Even where a "Christian line" is desirable at all—and that is a good deal rarer than many Christians think—developing a Christian line is impossible without first developing a Christian mind.

Expressed positively, thinking Christianly is thinking by Christians about anything and everything in a consistently Christian way—in a manner that is shaped, directed, and restrained by the truth of God's Word and God's Spirit.

As I use it, the phrase "thinking Christianly" is not as important as the idea it expresses. For thirty years many of us have followed Harry Blamires and found that "thinking Christianly" best captures the substance and spirit of what it means for the follower of Christ to grow in the mind of Christ. But others have used different phrases to express the same point—for example, "Christ-centered thinking," "biblical thinking," "developing a Christian mind," "thinking under the lordship of Christ," "lifelong learning under Christ," "developing a Christian world-and-lifeview," and so on.

What matters is not the term but the substance and spirit of the truth. Is it not absurd to affirm that Jesus Christ is Lord of all, the Alpha and the Omega, our creator, redeemer, and judge, the source, guide, and goal of all there is, and yet not be decisive over our minds and thinking? Evangelicals who rightly glory in all the new things in the gospel—a new birth, a new people, new powers, and a new age—must reinsert the vital, missing component of "new minds." Nowhere are the lordship of Christ and the power of the gospel more needed at the beginning and more glorious at the end.

Expressed differently by Ambassador Charles Malik, in all our thinking "the critic in the final analysis is Jesus Christ himself."[5] Thus " 'From the Christian point of view' has no solid foundation unless the word Christian here means Jesus Christ himself. So from the very start I have put aside all such questionable phraseology as 'from the Christian point of view,' 'in terms of Christian principles,' 'applying Christian principles or values,' 'from the standpoint of Christian culture,' etc."[6] The only question that finally counts is, What does Jesus think? Aside from that standard, all our thinking is "an exercise in fuzziness, in wobbly human effort, in subjectivist rationalism, in futility."[7]

What matters above all—whatever term we use—is that the idea and practice be kept simple, practical, and biblical. When all is said and done, the point is to love and obey God by loving him with our minds. For the Christian mind is a combination of intellectual light and spiritual ardor that, in Dorothy L. Sayers's term, is simply the "mind in love" with God.[8]

GOD-SENSE IS GOOD SENSE

The third step in reformation is to overcome the deepest of all obstacles to thinking Christianly. This is the incurable suspicion of thinking born of the distorted notion that, because divine wisdom is folly to human minds, Christian thinking is a contradiction in terms and it is therefore better to be irrational. From this perspective thinking Christianly is a fancy term for a futile exercise. Thinking Christianly, it is said, has no more chance than any other sort of thinking to rise above the folly that all human thinking amounts to when contrasted with God's wisdom. Far better, it is then claimed, to face this fact from the beginning and glory in the folly of not thinking—as an act of faithfulness.

This foolishness-as-faithfulness argument is evangelical anti-intellectualism at its deepest and most pious sounding. People who justify this notion commonly quote the Apostle Paul in his letter to Corinth: "For the message of the cross is folly to those who are perishing, but to us who are being saved it is the power of God. . . . For the foolishness of God is wiser than man's wisdom, and the weakness of God is stronger than man's strength."[9]

Such purported piety, however, is fallacious. For one thing, Christians who boast of "foolishness" overlook the relativity and irony in Paul's statement. The cross is certainly folly to those who are perishing—because their vantage point is wrong and their perspective distorted. Paul writes similarly in his second letter to Corinth that the very same messengers of the gospel are "the fragrance of life" to those being saved and "the smell of death" to those perishing. Thus when Paul writes of the gospel as "folly" he is being ironic. Objectively speaking, the gospel in itself is not folly but wisdom. Only in relation to a genuine folly foolish enough to pretend it is wise does true wisdom come to be seen and treated as folly.

Further, Christians who take a perverse pride in Christian foolishness overemphasize the fallenness of human thinking to the point of slandering Christ's work in creation and redemption. It is certainly true that "darkness" and "deceit" are defining features of the human mind under the influence of sin. Thus even Karl Marx, Sigmund Freud, and Jean-Paul Sartre in their respective views of "ideology," "rationalization," and "bad faith" are utopians in contrast with the biblical authors' realism about human thinking. But in the Scriptures the worst of the darkness and deceit is always offset by the grandeur of what the human mind was created to be and the glory of what it is redeemed to be again. Far from becoming humble compliments to the work of Christ, Christians who boast of folly insult its promise and achievement unwittingly.

Lastly, Christians who take a perverse pride in Christian foolishness confuse childishness with childlikeness, and thus irrationality with simplicity. True faith is unquestionably childlike and simple, but it is never childish or simplistic. St. Paul recognizes the former and echoes Jesus when he writes to the Christians in Ephesus: "Be imitators of God, therefore, as God's dear children." But being childlike does not imply being contented with immaturity. "Then we will no longer be infants. . ." he also writes. "Instead, speaking the truth in love, we will in all things grow up into him who is the Head, that is, Christ." St. Paul's conclusion carries us a long way from those who falsely boast of folly. "Be very careful, then, how you live—not as unwise but as wise" (or as another version puts it, "like sensible men, not like simpletons").[10]

Unless this fundamental distortion is tracked down and rooted out, it will become the deep spiritual root that grounds and nourishes other more recent distorting pressures. God-sense, as we shall see next, is nonsense to the world. In itself, however, it is good sense at its wisest, deepest, and most wholesome.

GOING MAD FOR GOD

The fourth step in reformation is to count the cost of discipleship entailed in thinking Christianly. For cost there is. The same truth that is good sense before God is nonsense to our world, which sees and sets itself over against God. The follower of Christ must therefore break with the world to be faithful to Christ. We must be prepared to bear with the world's folly.

Such "holy folly," or fool-bearing, is the proper understanding of Christian foolishness. It is as integral to thinking Christianly as it is to living Christianly. Russian orthodoxy, for example, has canonized thirty-six "holy fools." Blaise Pascal wrote: "Men are so inevitably mad that not to be mad would be to give a mad twist to madness."[11] G. K. Chesterton wrote similarly that a man who has faith must be prepared not only to be a martyr, but to be a fool. Far earlier Dante pronounced, in words that illuminate the cross of Jesus, the wisest person in the city is "He whom the fools hate worst."[12]

If this is true, some Christians have embraced folly of the wrong sort—boasting in what is literally foolish and becoming "fools proper." Others have made the equal but opposite mistake— of seeking to escape foolishness altogether, including the necessary scandal of the "foolbearer." Thus a common but false motivation for evangelical engagement in higher education is an overwhelming desire for respectability—as if academic success were a milestone of social mobility on the long, painful climb out of the intellectual slums of fundamentalism. Yet our Lord himself was dismissed as "mad" and "possessed," and the Apostle Paul was told by the Roman governor Festus that he was "out of his mind" because of his Christian thinking. We can expect no less.

The trick, of course, is not to delude ourselves about why we are called foolish. Not all folly is the fruit of faithfulness.

Sometimes when we are attacked as foolish we have quite simply been stupid and deserve the title we have earned. But in almost all generations and cultures, faithfulness will have some folly as its fruit. (Thomas Aquinas wrote of "good folly" and "evil wisdom," the former awarded for Christ's sake, the latter a sin.)

Knowing God and thinking Christianly is therefore a form of going mad for God. As the thirteenth-century Fransciscan lay-brother Iacopone da Todi wrote, "It seems to me great wisdom in a man if he wishes to go mad for God."[13] Or in the words of the Little Flower of Lisieux, "Now I have no other desire than to love Jesus even unto folly."[14]

NO AUTOMATIC PILOT

The fifth step in reformation is a commitment to thinking Christianly as a form of active obedience. Like every other part of the Christian life, thinking Christianly is active and demanding. It is neither easy nor automatic. St. Paul writes to the Corinthians that "we take captive every thought to make it obedient to Christ."[15] Thus thinking Christianly is inevitably moment by moment, question by question, issue by issue, point by point, and thought by thought. As Oswald Chambers wrote, "God will not make me think like Jesus, I have to do it myself; I have to bring every thought into captivity to the obedience of Christ."[16]

The basic possibilities are always stark: To think for oneself or to think for someone else; to think Christianly or to think un-Christianly. In terms of the first option, for example, John Maynard Keynes used to underscore the reminder: "Practical men, who believe themselves to be quite exempt from any intellectual influences, are usually the slaves of some defunct economist. Madmen in authority, who hear voices in the air, are distilling their frenzy from some academic scribbler of a few years back."[17]

In so far as the assumptions of any age differ from those of the gospel, they are the false assumptions that circulate in the air like latent heresies. Yet when someone becomes a Christian and either old assumptions are left over in his or her thinking or new assumptions are allowed in later, the result is not a mind made new but a patched-up mind. For alien assumptions, old or new, are like a Trojan horse in the city of the believer's mind.

If Christ's own disciples were guilty of thinking "as men think, not as God thinks," are we likely to do better? How do we know we are not thinking as Americans (or English, French, or Australians) think and not as God thinks? Have we checked that we are not closer to the twentieth-century (or sixteenth- or first-century) mind than the mind of Christ? Is our agenda closer to a liberal or conservative agenda than to the agenda of the kingdom of God? Are we more like the profile of Washingtonians (or New Yorkers, Los Angelenos, or Londoners) or of lawyers (or doctors and teachers) than of followers of Christ?

In each case the questions remind us that we are always worldlier and more culturally shortsighted than we realize. But the call of Jesus is radical. If our eyes offend us, pluck them out, he said. The same must be true of every intellectual assumption, authority, and conclusion that is closer to how humans think than the way God thinks. The search is on. The war has been declared. "All truth is God's truth," so we can welcome truth wherever it is to be found, even among pagans. But equally, "all that is not of God is not of truth" and therefore not for us, even if it is we who believe in it devoutly.

No, Not That Way

The sixth step in the reformation of evangelical thinking is to mark clearly the pitfalls and by-paths of Christian thinking. Put differently, thinking Christianly is not what it is often thought to be. Marking it clearly is important because pitfalls and by-paths are hazardous to those who fall in them and discouraging for those who witness the disaster.

Here are some common pitfalls and by-paths. One misconception concerns the idea that thinking Christianly is purely an intellectual activity—a "head trip" as it is often attacked. Far from it. As always the Bible addresses the heart as the center of the whole person and the understanding as the road to the whole person. The concept of "intellectual" in its modern sense of a person devoted to the nearly disembodied life of the mind is alien to the biblical understanding of human nature. Just as spiritual disciplines involve the body, so thinking Christianly engages the whole person. Modern intellectualism is as wrong and extreme as modern anti-intellectualism. Thinking Christianly is different from both. It engages us as whole people in the whole of life.

A second common misconception concerns the idea that thinking Christianly is purely an individual activity—as if August Rodin's "Penseur" (thinker) were wrapped in his heroic aloneness with a Bible in front of him. Again, far from it. The loneliness of the solitary genius was one of the false fruits of the nineteenth-century Romantic movement. These geniuses were considered especially heroic if they battled against impossible odds and died young. Thinking Christianly, however, is different. It is inescapably individual, as all discipleship is. But it is also inescapably collective. For all discipleship is communal because every disciple is part of the body of Christ.

Two particular parts of thinking Christianly require the collective dimension. One is the notion of the "corrigibility" of Christian thinking, in the sense that all of us need to be open to the correction of others to grow in wisdom. This was one reason why Charles Williams so treasured the stimulus of C. S. Lewis and other members of the Inklings discussion group. "Much was possible to a man in solitude," he wrote, "but some things were possible only to a man in companionship, and of these the most important was balance. No mind was so good that it did not need another mind to counter and equal it, and to save it from conceit and bigotry and folly."[18]

The other part of thinking Christianly that requires community is the notion of the "collegiality" of Christian thinking. For Christian thinking, like all Christian living, has a communal dimension. Enshrined in our word "college," which signifies a community of learning, the notion of collegiality in Christian thinking has become a cliché that in turn has been drowned by a tidal wave of individualism and specialization. In contrast, evangelical pietism originally gained its name from Spener's *collegiae pietatis* (colleges of piety). Both corrigibility and collegiality are captured in the well-known biblical proverb, "As iron sharpens iron, so one man sharpens the wits of another."[19]

A third common misconception concerns the idea that thinking Christianly is purely a human activity—as if to think is automatically to think purely in one's own strength and rely solely on one's own wits. Once again the opposite is true. Intellectualism is certainly a form of humanism because it concentrates on the human intellect in isolation from all else. And "Athens" has little to do with "Jerusalem" because of the place it gives to reason by itself. Christian thinking, in contrast, is anything but a purely human activity.

Thinking Christianly is premised only on the fear of the Lord that is the beginning of wisdom. Likewise, it proceeds only when we rely continually on God's word and Spirit. It always operates with the awareness of the supernatural source and dimensions of false thinking. As Paul writes to the Christians in Corinth, "For though we live in the world, we do not wage war as the world does. The weapons we fight with are not the weapons of this world. On the contrary, they have divine power to demolish strongholds. We demolish arguments and every pretension that sets itself up against the knowledge of God, and we take captive every thought to make it obedient to Christ."[20] Much of today's Christian scholarship would be transformed simply by returning to the classical notion of study as a spiritual discipline.

A fourth misconception concerns the idea that thinking Christianly is a form of uniformity—in other words, that if we all think Christianly we will all think the same way. When this happens, the goal of thinking Christianly collapses into a frantic search for the one particular correct way of thinking or acting. The result is the fallacy of "particularism," the uniformity of a particular "Christianly Correct" way of thinking.

Particularism, or the false ideal of uniformity, is under-standable as a reaction to the anything-goes pluralism of the other extreme. There thinking Christianly becomes synonymous with anything and everything that Christians think anyway. But particularism is equally extreme and equally fallacious because it denies two requirements of thinking Christianly that oppose all uniformity: the importance of diversity and the fact of human fallibility.

One form of particularism stems from a false desire for uni-formity in the realm of ideas. By virtue of being created in the image of God, all of us as human beings naturally desire coherent meaning. But by virtue of the Fall, we also have an added drive to debase coherence into systems of meaning that are centered on ourselves and closed to God. Thus even as Christians we are prone toward turning faith in God into a system of thought about God. In so doing we remove all mystery, tie up all the loose ends with our human logic, and finally reduce even Christ to being a mere part of our system of ideas.

The resulting systems of ideas—often purporting to be theologies—are empty and dead at best. At worst, they are dan-gerous and evil. For instead of Christ judging our human ideas, the name of Christ is made to justify our human ideas and coun-tersign our human endeavors, including ancient and modern crusades and inquisitions in his name.

The other, more common form of particularism stems from a false desire for uniformity in the realm of practice—the fallacy that if we all think Christianly we will all behave the same way. For one thing the idea itself is false. On the one hand, the com-munity of Christ is diverse, not uniform. Uniformity therefore denies the proper place of freedom and diversity. On the other hand, our highest accomplishments in this life are provisional, not final. Our best thinking and behavior is therefore not fully, finally Christian, but only more or less Christian than it was pre-viously.

For another thing, applying the idea of uniformity is disas-trous because it leads inevitably to legalism and judgmentalism.

There is only a short and easy step from "This is the Christian way" to "There is only one Christian way" to "Anything different from this way is not Christian" to "All those who differ from my way are not Christians." Far too many a letter from one Christian to another has begun in reality or in spirit, "Dear former brother/sister in Christ."

The fallacy of particularism stems from the fact that God has not spoken definitively to us about everything. Obviously he did not intend to. Thus if it is an error for some Christians to make relative what God has made absolute, it is equally an error for others to make absolute what God has left relative. Put differently, where God has not spoken definitively we can legitimately say "This conclusion (or policy or lifestyle) is *not* Christian." But it is not legitimate to go further and say, "This conclusion (or policy or lifestyle) *alone* is Christian."

We must all think Christianly, but for that very reason we must not all think the same way. There is no one Christian form of politics any more than there is one Christian form of poetry, raising a family, or planning a retirement. Again, many ways are definitely *not* Christian, but no *one* way alone is. Diversity rather than uniformity is a direct consequence of Christian freedom as well as Christian fallibility. Helmut Thielicke, the German theologian and ethicist, was right to ask, "Do we not have to respect the fact that under the shadow of forgiveness different decisions are possible and different liberties and loyalties may exist?"[21]

Unless these four pitfalls are marked off, they are guaranteed to be a snare to the renewal of Christian thinking. Thinking Christianly is distorted not only by those who do not take it seriously, but also by those who take it seriously but in a wrong direction.

KNOWING MEANS DOING

The seventh step in reformation is to focus attention on a long-neglected part of Christian thinking—developing a Christian thought-style. This emphasis may appear strange because thinking Christianly is thought to be opposed to style in a double sense.

On the one hand, style (as we saw in Part Two) has become so detached from substance that it is all a matter of images and appearance. From the perspective of such a critical stance toward modern style, the current buzzword "lifestyle" is dubious enough. To introduce a new notion of "thought-style," as if Christians should be concerned with appearances, seems even worse. On the other hand, thinking Christianly is almost never associated with thought-style. Where it is not restricted to purely theological truths, it is usually extended only in the direction of philosophical premises and all that it means to develop a Christian world-and-life-view. But anyone who studies the biblical understanding of knowledge and knowing soon realizes that God determines how we think as well as what we think. In the classical sense of style as the external expression of inner character, Christian thinking has its own characteristic style as much as content.

A full exposition of Christian thought-style would require a book in itself. For example, we have already noted in passing two of the defining features of the Christian thought-style—collegiality and corrigibility. Other obvious ones include the certainty, humility, spirituality, rationality, mystery, and intensity of Christian knowing. But one of the most decisive features—and one directly opposed to modern styles of thinking—is the biblical insistence on the responsibility of knowing.

Modern knowledge is characteristically noncommittal. Much is known, but all is consequence-free. What we know and what we do about it are two different things. Various roots of this noncommittal style of knowing could be explored. Philosophically, for example, the Anglo-Saxon world in the twentieth century has been dominated by what John Dewey described well as "the spectator theory of knowledge." Owing to the triumph of such forces as empiricism and science, the myth is prevalent that knowledge is objective, universal, and certain—and therefore neutral, detached, impersonal, noninvolving and nonresponsible. What we do with what we know has nothing to do with knowing itself.

Other factors have reinforced the noncommittal character of modern knowledge. An obvious one is the impossible overload of modern information. Another is the essentially detached style of the media—epitomized by Christopher Isherwood's famous but absurd line in A Berlin Diary, "I am a camera with its shutter open, quite passive, recording, not thinking."[22]

Another obvious factor is bureaucracy. This has become a process of specialization through which the rise of specialists, technicians, and experts has led to a dual loss: of the sense of the wider whole and of the responsibility of the individual for anything other than his or her own part. But when all possible factors are taken into account—from ethics and psychology and so on—the result is the disastrously irresponsible way of knowing that characterizes the so-called information era. Never has more been known; never has less been required of what is known. From abstract mathematical formulas to anguishing international atrocities, the common reaction to modern knowledge is, So what? Who cares? What do you expect me to do?

We could argue that this response is philosophically unwarranted—that in fact responsibility is an inescapable assumption of all human knowing. But this point is stronger for the follower of Christ who is committed to thinking Christianly. For what is at best a small assumption of the better modern philosophy is a central assertion of Christian theology.

The Christian idea of the responsibility of knowledge is rooted in the notion that God is there and that he speaks. He is therefore the one with both the first decisive word on life—in creation—and the last decisive word—in judgment. Thus human life is essentially responsible, answerable, and accountable. Such responsibility of knowledge is the silent assumption in many basic doctrines. Sin, for example, is a deliberate violation of the responsibility of knowledge—human beings become responsible where they should not be (playing God) and refuse to be responsible where they should be (denying guilt).

This responsibility of knowledge is also embedded in the root meaning of many of the biblical words. For example, the Hebrew word "to know" includes the meaning "to care for." The idea is that "knowledge of" something is "power over" it, "responsibility to" it, and "care for" it. Thus when the Proverbs say that "A righteous man cares for his beast, but a wicked man is cruel at heart,"[23] the Hebrew word "cares" is actually "knows." It signifies that a righteous person has a caring knowledge that responsibly treats his animal with integrity—that is, true to the truth of what it is before God. The wicked person, by contrast, understands all knowledge in relation only to himself or herself rather than to God and therefore "understands no such concern."

We can see the biblical understanding of the responsibility of knowledge supremely in Jesus. For where the first man, Adam, severed the link between knowledge and responsibility, the second Adam reunited them. Refusing the devil's temptations to make claims that had no consequences, Jesus set his face toward Jerusalem and the cross. The responsibility of his knowing who he was and what he had come to do marked his way to his death.

Needless to say, what matters for our thought-style is not simply doctrine but the Christian responsibility of knowledge exhibited in all our knowing. Possible applications are myriad—in our attitudes to education, careers, specialization, elitism, cynicism, resistance to evil, and a score of different areas. But the recurring motif is the costly obedience of Christian knowing. Knowledge for the Christian is never noncommittal nor consequence-free. Knowledge carries responsibility. Knowing means doing. What we do with what we know is what Christian knowing is all about—and the responsibility of knowledge is only one example of the importance of Christian thought-style.

THE DEFENSE NEVER RESTS

The eighth step in reformation is to recover the practice of Christian apologetics, or of making a persuasive case for the Christian faith for today's generation. Apologetics has usually held an honored, if controversial, place throughout Christian history. Most of the great theologians—including Paul, Origen, Augustine, Aquinas, and Calvin—have also been unashamed apologists for the Christian faith. Benjamin Warfield even claimed that the Christian faith "stands out among all religions, therefore, as distinctly 'the Apologetick religion.' "[24] Evangelicals today, however, display a troubling ignorance and unease about apologetics. As stressed earlier, the lack of a powerful, contemporary evangelical apology is one of the four great facts of our shame and a key part of the persuasionlessness that has befallen us. Where we meet people who are open, interested, and needy, we are ready to share our faith because most of our methods of witnessing assume that people are so. But when we find people who are not open, interested, or needy, we are stuck—though we mask our impotence by the compensating vehemence of our proclamation (or in the political arena by our protest and picketing).

Thus ironically, evangelicals now collude with liberals against traditional Christian apologetics. Whereas the broad liberal tendency of the past half century has been to say, "Don't defend, dialogue," the broad conservative tendency has been to say, "Don't persuade, proclaim." As philosopher Antony Flew lamented a generation ago, "Belief cannot argue with unbelief: It can only preach to it."[25]

Caught in this pincer-like grip, traditional apologetics has commonly been rejected or neglected. What remains is all too limited and contained. Sometimes, as I said, apologetics today is limited to addressing the open and interested—a shrinking audience in a society growing increasingly secular in public life and pluralistic in private life. Sometimes it is limited to addressing the needy—as if, as Peter Berger wrote, "the necessary counterpoint of the Christian proclamation was an anthropology of desperation."[26] Sometimes it is limited to addressing rational, literary, abstract, middle-class thinkers—so that, as critics have said, our style appeals mainly to the more complicated heirs of a Christian culture and education who are by that very fact more likely to be closed to our message.

Worst of all, evangelical apologetics today is frequently contained in Christian circles—so that entire courses are given and weighty books written and debated that never in a million years will touch real flesh-and-blood nonbelievers. As one professor of apologetics said to me of his eminent predecessor at a well-known evangelical seminary, "He taught people how to teach apologetics, not to do it."

The present moment is truly the hour for authentic Christian apologetics. On the one hand, the outlook in some directions is sobering. As evangelical churches grow careless about orthodoxy, instances of heresy, blasphemy, and nonsense are mounting. As modern society grows increasingly secular in some spheres of life and pluralistic in others, powerful alternatives to the gospel are proliferating. Similarly, as modern life calls into question more and more of what it means to be fundamentally human—including such requirements as personal identity, truth, and stable families—society's questions and crises mount year by year. On the other hand, the outlook in other directions is encouraging. If the church is in disarray, the church's opponents are in even greater disarray. Pre-Christian rivals to the gospel, such as full-blooded, old-fashioned paganism, may be somewhat resurgent. But the post-Christian rivals to the gospel—such as humanism and secularism, not to mention Marxism and Freudianism—are at a lower ebb than at any time in the past four hundred years.

The time has come for evangelicals to wake from our lethargy or turn from our fear, blaming, and victim-playing. We must move out into all spheres of society, presenting the case for the gospel of Jesus in ways that are fresh, powerful, imaginative, compassionate, and persuasive. A sure sign of a genuine reformation of our appalling anti-intellectualism will be the rise of a new generation of Christian apologists.

FOR GOD'S SAKE

The immense project of going beyond the initial reformation of evangelical thinking to recapturing the great establishments of modern thought lies far beyond this slim volume. We have looked at only half, though perhaps the harder half, of what Charles Malik called the two tasks—"the twofold miracle of evangelizing the great universities and intellectualizing the great Evangelical movement."[27] But our challenge is to begin. I would add one last spur.

One of the greatest sadnesses of a thinking evangelical is knowing the thousands who have left, and are still leaving, evangelicalism because evangelicals do not think. It was not always so. We have noted the Puritans. Similarly the evangelicals around William Wilberforce were described as a group "whose brains and brilliancy would not be denied even by those who sneered at their religion."[28] To be sure, the defections have been more than offset by the fruits of our witnessing. Even today the thousands who have left evangelicalism for Catholicism and Eastern Orthodoxy, or—far worse—for agnosticism and atheism, are greatly outnumbered by the millions who are becoming evangelical worldwide.

But both the number and caliber of those who have left are a terrible indictment of our anti-intellectualism—made more poignant still in the case of our own friends and contemporaries. The story of the young evangelical Edmund Gosse from a century ago illustrates this terrible poignancy. He was the son of Philip Gosse, a distinguished evangelical biologist and friend of T. H. Huxley. But finally the underlying anti-intellectualism of evangelicalism confronted his independence and he wrote:

> When such defiance is offered to the intelligence of a thoughtful and honest young man with the natural impulses of his twenty-one years, there are but two alternatives. Either he must cease to think for himself; or his individualism must be instantly confirmed and the necessity of religious independence must be emphasized.
>
> No compromise, as is seen, was offered; no proposal of a truce would have been acceptable. It was a case of "Everything or Nothing"; and thus desperately challenged, the young man's conscience threw off once for all the yoke of his "dedication," and, as respectfully as he could, without parade or remonstrance, he took a human being's privilege to fashion his inner life for himself.[29]

Nearer our own time the writer Dorothy L. Sayers is another who self-consciously rejected evangelicalism because of its anti-intellectualism. Her time at the Godolphin School in Surrey, England, left her with a distaste for evangelical pietism. There were two kinds of Christian faith, she concluded. The pietistic and evangelical was sentimental and made her feel uncomfortable; the other appealed openly to the understanding. "The cultivation of religious emotion without philosophic basis," she explained, "is thoroughly pernicious."[30] Her evangelical schooling, she reflected later, was simply a period for "gawky young souls growing out of their spiritual clothing."[31]

When we ponder such stories and the thousands of people who feel they have had to shed their evangelical clothing, is it not time for anger or tears? This book is not meant to be an academic exercise. It is a cry from the heart for thought, debate, prayer, action, and reformation. One of the great legacies for those of us who knew the late Francis Schaeffer was that truth mattered to him. He took God seriously, he took people seriously, and he took truth seriously. Friedrich Nietzsche's aphorism could be applied to him, "All truths are bloody truths to me."

Golda Meir, Prime Minister of Israel, wrote a moving account of the debate in the Knesset after the Yom Kippur war. The speeches of the opposition tore her apart, she said. They were so full of rhetoric and theatricality that she could not stand it. When the time came to close the debate, she refused to reply. "I just want to say one thing," she said. "I want to quote a very dear friend of mine . . . who once attended a debate on some very serious matter—though it wasn't nearly as serious as what we are talking about here and now—and a man got up to speak. He spoke so effortlessly and easily that all my friend could say was: 'If only he had stammered or hesitated occasionally.' "[32]

Perhaps as we ponder the length and breadth of our anti-intellectualism, as we survey its consequences, as we remember its casualties, and as we meditate on its core disloyalty to our Lord, it is time for us to stammer and hesitate—and seek God's help to change our minds and our ways of thinking.

NOTES

Introduction: A Scandal and a Sin

1. Friedrich Nietzsche, *Thus Spake Zarathustra*, trans. Walter Kaufmann (London: Penguin, 1978), pp. 17–18.
2. Charles Malik, *The Two Tasks* (Downers Grove, Ill.: InterVarsity, 1980), p. 33.
3. Harry Blamires, *The Christian Mind* (London: SPCK, 1963), pp. vii, 3.
4. Alistair Cooke, *The Patient Has the Floor* (New York: Knopf, 1986), p. 12.
5. John Schaar, "A Nation of Behavers," *The New York Review of Books*, 22 October 1976, p. 6.
6. See James Davison Hunter, *American Evangelicalism* (New Brunswick, N.J.: Rutgers, 1983), pp. 53–54.
7. See *The Williamsburg Charter Survey on Religion and Public Life* (Washington, D.C.: The Williamsburg Charter Foundation, 1988).
8. Paul Johnson, *Intellectuals* (New York: HarperPerennial, 1990), p. 342.

Part One: A Ghost Mind

1. Alexis de Tocqueville, *Democracy in America*, vol. I (New York: Vintage, 1945), p. 43.
2. Quoted in Sydney E. Ahlstrom, *A Religious History of the American People*, vol. I (Garden City, N.Y.: Image, 1975), p. 198.

3. Richard Hofstadter, *Anti-Intellectualism in American Life* (New York: Vintage, 1962), p. 59.

Chapter 1: Polarization

1. Quoted in Richard J. Mouw, *Uncommon Decency* (Downers Grove, Ill.: InterVarsity, 1992), p. 145.
2. Quoted in Hofstadter, *Anti-Intellectualism in American Life*, p. 67.
3. Quoted in Nathan O. Hatch, *The Democratization of American Christianity* (New Haven, Conn.: Yale, 1989), p. 89.
4. Hofstadter, *Anti-Intellectualism in American Life*, p. 97.
5. L. Frank Baum, *The Wonderful Wizard of Oz* (New York: Dover, 1960), pp. 57–58, 61.
6. Hofstadter, *Anti-Intellectualism in American Life*, p. 45.
7. Ibid., p. 46.
8. Ibid., p. 47.
9. Ibid., p. 87.
10. Quoted in ibid., p. 96.
11. Quoted in ibid., p. 122.
12. Quoted in ibid., p. 129.
13. Charles Malik, *The Two Tasks* (Downers Grove, Ill.: InterVarsity, 1980), p. 32.

Chapter 2: Pietism

1. See George Huntemann, *The Other Bonhoeffer*, trans. Todd Huizinga (Grand Rapids, Mich.: Baker, 1993), p. 101.
2. Theodore Roszak, *Where the Wasteland Ends* (New York: Doubleday, 1973), p. 449.
3. F. R. Cossitt, *Life and Times of Rev. Finis Ewing* (Louisville, Ky.: Board of Publications of Cumberland Presbyterian Church, 1853), p. 14.
4. Quoted in Sydney E. Ahlstrom, *A Religious History of the American People* (Garden City, N.Y.: Image, 1975), pp. 500–501.
5. Quoted in Ahlstrom, *A Religious History of the American People*, vol. II, p. 153.
6. Quoted in Hofstadter, *Anti-Intellectualism in American Life*, p. 108.
7. Quoted in Ahlstrom, *A Religious History of the American People*, vol. II, p. 204.

8. Quoted in William G. McLoughlin, *Billy Sunday Was His Real Name* (Chicago: University of Chicago Press, 1955), p. 123.

Chapter 3: Primitivism

1. Speech to the U.S. Chamber of Commerce, 21 April 1986.
2. Richard T. Hughes and C. Leonard Allen, *Illusions of Innocence: Protestant Primitivism in America 1693–1875* (Chicago: University of Chicago Press, 1988), p. 15.
3. Ibid., p. 25.
4. Ibid., p. 13.
5. Alexis de Tocqueville, *Democracy in America*, ed. J. P. Mayer, trans. George Lawrence (Garden City, N.Y.: Doubleday, 1969), p. 508.
6. Quoted in Hughes and Allen, *Illusions of Innocence*, p. 57.

Chapter 4: Populism

1. Hatch, *The Democratization of American Christianity*, p. 211.
2. Quoted in ibid., p. 67.
3. Quoted in ibid., p. 179.
4. Quoted in Mark A. Noll, *The Scandal of the Evangelical Mind* (Grand Rapids, Mich.: Eerdmans, 1994), p. 128.
5. Quoted in Hatch, p. 69.
6. Quoted in ibid., p. 19.
7. Quoted in ibid., p. 215.

Chapter 5: Pluralism

1. Quoted in Philip Rieff, *The Triumph of the Therapeutic* (Chicago: University of Chicago Press, 1987), p. 83.
2. Peter L. Berger, "Capitalism and the Disordering of Modernity," *First Things*, January 1991, p. 9.
3. John Murray Cuddihy, *No Offense* (New York: Seabury, 1978), pp. 1–2.
4. Alexis de Tocqueville, Letter to Alexis de Kergolay, 29 June 1831.
5. Quoted in Martin E. Marty, *A Nation of Believers* (Chicago: University of Chicago Press, 1976), p. 201.

Chapter 6: Pragmatism

1. Quoted in Hofstadter, *Anti-Intellectualism in American Life*, p. 267.
2. Norman Vincent Peale, *A Guide to Confident Living* (New York: Prentice-Hall: 1948), p. 46.
3. William G. McLoughlin, ed., *Lectures on Revivals of Religion* (Cambridge: Harvard, 1960), p. 12
4. For a fuller description, see Os Guinness, *Dining with the Devil: The Megachurch Movement Flirts with Modernity* (Grand Rapids, Mich.: Baker, 1993).

Chapter 7: Philistinism

1. Quoted in Hofstadter, *Anti-Intellectualism in American Life*, p. 119.
2. Quoted in ibid., p. 122.
3. Frequently quoted in Wheaton College classes by the late Dr. Clyde Kilby.
4. Quoted in Hofstadter, *Anti-Intellectualism in American Life*, p. 94.

Chapter 8: Premillenialism

1. Noll, *The Scandal of the Evangelical Mind*, p. 114.

Part Two: An Idiot Culture

1. Tchiyuka Cornelius, quoted in Mary Jordan, "Colleges Must Admit: Applications Swerving to the Zany Side," *Washington Post*, 8 April 1994, p. A1; "Give Me an A, or Give Me Death," *Newsweek*, 13 June 1994, p. 62.
2. Carl Bernstein, "The Idiot Culture," *The New Republic*, 8 June 1992, pp. 24–25.
3. See, for example, Guinness, *Dining with the Devil*.
4. Quoted in Neil Postman, *Amusing Ourselves to Death* (New York: Viking, 1985), p. 34.
5. George Steiner, *Extraterritorial* (Harmondsworth: Penguin, 1968), p. 168.
6. Ibid.
7. Noll, *The Scandal of the Evangelical Mind*, pp. 113–114.
8. Irenaeus, *Against Heresies*, I.8.3.

Chapter 9: Amusing Ourselves to Death

1. See Postman, *Amusing Ourselves to Death*.
2. Ibid., p. 4.
3. Ibid., pp. 92–93.
4. Quoted in *Wall Street Journal*, 7 May 1986, p. 1.
5. Postman, *Amusing Ourselves to Death*, p. 107.
6. Ibid., p. 99.
7. Quoted in ibid., p. 137.
8. Quoted in Jacques Ellul, *Technological Bluff*, p. 339.
9. From a speech delivered in October 1985 to the International Radio and Television Society, New York City.

Chapter 10: People of Plenty

1. Peter Carlson, "It's an Ad, Ad, Ad, Ad World," *Washington Post Magazine*, 3 November 1991, p. 15.
2. See David M. Potter, *People of Plenty* (Chicago: University of Chicago Press, 1954).
3. Quoted in Douglas T. Miller and Marion Novak, *The Fifties: The Way We Were* (Garden City, N.Y.: Doubleday, 1977), p. 117.
4. Potter, *People of Plenty*, p. 183.

Chapter 11: All Consuming Images

1. Stuart Ewen, *All Consuming Images: The Politics of Style in Contemporary Culture* (New York: Basic Books, 1988).
2. Quoted in ibid., p. 25.
3. Ibid., p. 25.
4. Quoted in ibid., p. 43.
5. Quoted in Debora Silverman, *Selling Culture* (New York: Pantheon, 1986), pp. 108, 119, 155.
6. Quoted in Ewen, *All Consuming Images*, p. 30.
7. See ibid., pp. 260–261.
8. See Os Guinness, *The American Hour* (New York: Free Press, 1993), pp. 290–303.
9. Quoted in ibid., p. 291.

Chapter 12: The Humiliation of the Word

1. Henri M. Nouwen, "Silence, the Portable Cell," *Sojourners*, July 1980, p. 22.
2. Ellul, *The Humiliation of the Word*, p. 204.
3. "She Wants her TV! He Wants his Book!" *Harper's*, March 1991, p. 47.
4. Isaac Asimov, "Your Future as a Writer," *Writer's Digest*, May 1986, p. 26.
5. Ibid.
6. Ibid.
7. Ibid.
8. David J. Wolpe, *In Speech and in Silence: The Jewish Quest for God* (New York: Henry Holt, 1992), p. 77.
9. Steiner, *Extraterritorial*, pp. 68, 108.
10. Wolpe, *In Speech and in Silence*, p. 78.
11. Ellul, *The Humiliation of the Word*, p. 254.
12. Quoted in Perry D. LeFevre, ed., *The Prayers of Kierkegaard* (Chicago: University of Chicago, 1956), p. 132.
13. "She Wants her TV! He Wants his Book!" p. 47.
14. Ellul, *The Humiliation of the Word*, p. 269.

Chapter 13: Cannibals of PoMo

1. Quoted in Ewen, *All Consuming Images*, pp. 33–34.
2. James Dobson, "Immorality in the Media," Focus on the Family broadcast, 26 October 1992.
3. Quoted in Jo Ann Lewis, "It's Postmodern and If You Don't Get It You Don't Get It," *Washington Post*, 27 March 1994, p. G6.
4. Quoted in Silverman, *Selling Culture*, pp. 16–17.

Chapter 14: Tabloid Truth

1. David Nakamura, "TV Host 'Went too Far,' " *Washington Post*, 8 April 1994, p. B3.
2. Ibid.
3. Carl Bernstein, "The Idiot Culture," p. 28.
4. Henry Fairlie, *The Seven Deadly Sins Today* (Notre Dame, Ind.: Notre Dame Press, 1979), pp. 65–66.

5. William Lee Miller, *The First Liberty* (New York: Knopf, 1986), p. 72.
6. See, for example, Joshua Shenk, "Limbaugh's Lies: Anatomy of a Yarn Spinner," *The New Republic*, 24 May 1994, p. 12.
7. Garrison Keillor, "From Lake Woebegon to Whitewater," *Washington Post*, 17 April 1994, p. C7.
8. 2 Corinthians 10:4.
9. 1 Peter 3:15.
10. Quoted in Bernard Crick, *George Orwell: A Life* (Harmondsworth: Penguin, 1980), p. 326.
11. Quoted in Hank Hanegraaff, *Christianity in Crisis* (Eugene, Oreg.: Harvest House, 1993), p. 336.
12. Quoted in ibid.
13. Quoted in ibid.

Chapter 16: Real, Reel, or Virtually Real?

1. John Schwartz, "A Terminal Obsession," *Washington Post*, 27 March 1994, p. F4.
2. Michael Heim, *The Metaphysics of Virtual Reality* (New York: Oxford University Press, 1993), p. 38.
3. Ibid., p. 131.
4. Matie Molinaro, Corrine McLuhan, and William Toye, eds., *The Letters of Marshall McLuhan* (New York: Oxford University Press, 1987), p. 406.
5. "Mailer's Lament," *Washington Post Book World*, 8 May 1994, p. 15.
6. Romans 12:2.

Part Three: Let My People Think

1. Postman, *Amusing Ourselves to Death*, p. 59.
2. Ibid., p. 126.
3. Dorothy L. Sayers, "The Lost Tools of Learning," *National Review*, 19 January 1979, p. 91.
4. Mark 8:33, NEB.
5. Charles Habib Malik, *A Christian Critique of the University* (Downers Grove, Ill.: InterVarsity, 1982), p. 23.
6. Ibid., p. 25.
7. Ibid., p. 27.

8. Quoted in Barbara Reynolds, *Dorothy L. Sayers: Her Life and Soul* (New York: St. Martin's Press, 1993), p. 368.
9. 1 Corinthians 1:18, 25.
10. Ephesians 4:14–15; 5:15.
11. Blaise Pascal, *Penseés*, trans. A. J. Krailsheimer (Harmondsworth: Penguin, 1966), p. 148.
12. Quoted in Henry F. May, *Ideas, Faiths, and Feelings* (Oxford: Oxford University Press, 1983), p. 15.
13. Quoted in John Saward, *Perfect Fools* (Oxford: Oxford University Press, 1980), p. 89.
14. Quoted in ibid., p. 211.
15. 2 Corinthians 10:5.
16. Oswald Chambers, *My Utmost for His Highest*, June 14 (New York: Dodd, Mead and Company, 1935), p. 166.
17. John Maynard Keynes, *The General Theory of Employment Interest and Money* (London: Macmillan, 1936), p. 383.
18. Quoted in Humphrey Carpenter, *The Inklings* (London: George Allen & Unwin, 1978), p. 117.
19. Proverbs 27:17, NEB.
20. 2 Corinthians 10:3–5.
21. Helmut Thielicke, *Theological Ethics*, vol. I (Grand Rapids, Mich.: Eerdmans, 1979) p. 622.
22. Quoted in Crick, *George Orwell: A Life*, p. 166.
23. Proverbs 12:10, NEB.
24. Benjamin B. Warfield, "Introductory Note" in Francis R. Beattie, *A Treatise on Apologetics*, vol. I (Richmond, Va.: The Presbyterian Committee of Publication, 1903), p. 26.
25. Antony Flew, *God and Politics* (London: Hutchinson, 1966), p. 9.
26. Peter L. Berger, *A Rumor of Angels* (New York: Anchor, 1970), p. 68.
27. Malik, *The Two Tasks*, p. 35.
28. Quoted in Ernest Marshall Howse, *Saints in Politics* (London: George Allen & Unwin, 1952), pp. 24–25.
29. Edmund Gosse, *Father and Son* (London: The Filio Society, 1972), p. 225.
30. Quoted in Reynolds, *Dorothy L. Sayers*, p. 38.
31. Ibid., p. 58.
32. Golda Meir, *My Life* (New York: Dell, 1976), p. 434.